Victim Support Handbook

Helping People
Cope with Crime

Editor: Philippa Spackman

Hodder & Stoughton

Acknowledgements

Victim Support would like to thank the very many people within Victim Support and other organisations, as well as the victims whose experience informs all of the charity's work, for their help in making this book possible.

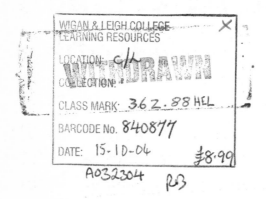

Orders: please contact Bookpoint Ltd, 78 Milton Park, Abingdon, Oxon OX14 4TD. Telephone: (44) 01235 827720, Fax: (44) 01235 400454. Lines are open from 9.00–6.00, Monday to Saturday, with a 24 hour message answering service. Email address: orders@bookpoint.co.uk

British Library Cataloguing in Publication Data
A catalogue record for this title is available from The British Library

ISBN 0 340 780495

First published 2000
Impression number   10   9   8   7   6   5   4   3   2   1
Year   2005   2004   2003   2002   2001   2000

Typeset by Transet Limited, Coventry, England.
Printed in Great Britain for Hodder & Stoughton Educational, a division of Hodder Headline plc, 338 Euston Road, London NW1 3BH by Cox & Wyman Ltd, Reading, Berkshire.

Contents

Victim Support has 25 years' experience in helping people cope with crime. For some victims, crime is nothing more than an inconvenience – an insurance form to fill in or a lock to be mended. For others, however, the effects are severe and long-lasting.

The aim of this book is to pass on some of what Victim Support has learned about how people react to crime. To pass this on to victims, their families and friends, as well as to other people from whom victims might seek help, or who might come into contact with victims in the course of their work. Among the many people who fall into this category are members of parliament, ministers of religion, local councillors, community leaders, police officers, social workers, doctors, housing officers, trade union officers, lawyers and teachers.

The first two chapters of the book describe the emotional impact of crime and, for those who report crimes to the police, what happens during the police investigation and criminal justice process. Following chapters consider five main areas of crime, from homicide to sexual violence, other crimes against people, crimes against property and crimes involving children. Each of these describes how victims may react, what official procedures may follow such crimes and what other people can do to help. The book concludes by providing contact details for other organisations who also work with victims of crime.

The word 'victim' is used in the book as shorthand for anyone who has suffered as a result of crime. This is not intended to suggest that people do not get over crime and remain in that state for ever – most come to terms with what has happened and carry on with their lives. But it is when people are in the aftermath of crime, as victims, that Victim Support is closest to them, providing them with practical help and emotional support to enable them to move on. It is therefore our experience of what it means to be a 'victim' that is offered here.

This book is mainly about crimes against individuals by individuals. While this includes crimes such as robbery, which may be committed against people while they are at work, it does not cover crimes for which commercial or other organisations may be responsible, for example, industrial or environmental accidents, or cases of medical or corporate negligence. Nor does it cover other events that may have serious or even fatal consequences for the victim and their family, for example, natural disasters, cot death and suicide. The traumas that people suffer from these are also very great, but our primary task is to deal with the consequences of crimes.

This book may be unique: we hope people will buy it for the information it contains, while never needing to put that information to use. But if someone you know becomes a victim of crime and needs your support, we hope this book will help you to help them. You can also call the Victim Supportline on lo-call number 0845 30 30 900 and speak to someone, who can in addition put you in touch with your local Victim Support scheme.

Dame Helen Reeves DBE, Chief Executive of Victim Support

Overview

- Victim Support
- How crime affects people
- Victims' reactions
  - Initial reactions
  - Recovering
  - Moving on
- Factors which affect victims' recovery
- The financial effects of crime
- Repeat and secondary victimisation
- Vulnerable people and crime
- Other people's reactions
  - The ripple effect
  - Sparing the grief
  - Over-protection
  - Guilt and anger
- How you can help

Victim Support

Victim Support is an independent voluntary organisation and national charity, which exists solely for the purpose of helping people cope with the complex and confusing consequences of crime.

Every year trained volunteers and staff in branches throughout England, Wales and Northern Ireland work with thousands of people who have suffered crimes, such as burglary, sexual assault, domestic violence, racist violence, theft, or even the violent death of a loved one. Sister organisations work with victims in Scotland and the Republic of Ireland.

Offering victims emotional support and practical assistance in complete confidence, free of charge, Victim Support will help people for as long as it takes them to recover from the effects of the crime, including offering them support, through its Witness Service, if they have to give evidence in court.

Victims are usually referred to Victim Support by the police, but victims do not have to have reported a crime to the police for Victim Support to offer them its services. Victims can contact Victim Support themselves, for example, by calling the Victim Supportline on lo-call number 0845 30 30 900, or by looking in the telephone directory to find the contact details for their local scheme.

How crime affects people

Everyone reacts differently to crime. Reactions vary according to the type of crime and the circumstances of the victim at the time it happens. While some people are able to get on with their lives immediately, others can take weeks, months or years to begin to pick up the pieces, or talk about the effect that the crime has had on them.

Not every victim will experience the range of reactions covered in this book. However, Victim Support has learned that there are some common responses to crime and some common approaches to supporting victims. It is that understanding of the impact of crime, and how victims can be helped to cope with its effects, which this book sets out to share.

One reason why crimes are so difficult for victims to come to terms with is that most have been deliberately caused by another person who has wilfully intruded into the victim's life. As a result, many victims feel they have suffered a fundamental loss of control in addition to other losses that may be involved, for example, physical and financial losses, as well as losses of confidence in society, self-esteem, or loss of faith in others.

The impact of crime may be psychological, physiological, behavioural, financial or practical. Whether or not the crime is officially recorded as such by the police, someone who believes and feels that they have been offended against may suffer one or more of these effects.

For some people, for example, the impact of burglary amounts to no more than the practical tasks of notifying the police and completing an insurance claim form. Others, however, may feel violated, because strangers have intruded in their personal lives. In addition, they may feel that the loss of irreplaceable possessions of sentimental value carries such psychological weight that their experience of burglary is similar to that of a bereavement.

For those who cannot afford to take out insurance, the loss of household goods causes considerable financial hardship. Victims may also feel profoundly insecure, fearing that the burglars will come back and that their home is no longer safe. In response, they may turn their home into a fortress and withdraw from social contact to try to protect themselves and their possessions. Such feelings can in turn lead to the practical and costly effect of victims having to move house to try to regain their peace of mind.

All these are normal reactions to abnormal events. Regardless of how serious the crime appears to the onlooker, if a victim is distressed by crime, it matters to them and other people should respond accordingly.

Victims' reactions

Initial reactions

Victim Support recognises various stages in the process of responding to crime. A victim's first reaction is often not to believe that a crime has been committed at all, and feel it couldn't or shouldn't have happened to them. They may be shocked and disorientated and in a state of panic or frenzy, for a moment or for a longer period of time. They may also feel frightened and helpless. They may cry, shake and feel both physically sick and emotionally violated by the crime.

Guilt is also a common reaction. Some victims tell themselves that the crime might not have happened if they had acted differently, for example, by checking all the doors and windows or taking a different route home. But even if they did leave a window open or walk home alone at night, that did not entitle someone else to ransack their home or attack them. Whatever the victim did and however they responded, they did the right thing for them at the time and the offender is the only person responsible for the crime.

Anger is another frequent early response to crime. The anger may be exhibited in swearing, shouting or other aggressive behaviour, and it may be directed towards the offender or displaced onto someone else. If a victim feels anger or any other emotion, that is simply the way they feel and they need not apologise for it. Having someone to talk to, in confidential surroundings, can help them to deal with their feelings.

These initial reactions are often followed by longer term and more complex emotions, which might include psychological, physiological or behavioural responses. Examples of these might be nightmares, depression, weeping, having intrusive thoughts about the event, loss of confidence, inability to sleep, difficulty in eating, headaches, nausea and increased smoking or drinking. Victims may feel bitter, confused, shattered, frustrated, dirty or insecure, and become obsessive, rebel against constraints or experience revenge fantasies.

Victims may also withdraw from family and wider social contacts, feeling restricted in their ability to go to work or study, or to carry on with their normal daily life. They may feel it is too dangerous to go out and be unwilling to leave the house alone or after dark or to leave the house unattended. Distrust of both strangers and of people who are close to them may result in victims having difficulties in their relationships. At the most fundamental level, their belief in a just and stable world may have been shattered.

Recovering

A crucial stage in the victim's recovery is when they come to accept the reality of what has happened. They may still feel vulnerable and fragile, and still be wary and hesitant, but by this time they are no longer blaming themselves or wishing to turn the clock back. They may begin to reconstruct their lives, and both acknowledge the crime and take precautions to try to ensure it does not happen again.

In this way, people begin to make sense of their experience, often by seeking and receiving help from other people. They may even evaluate the event as leading to personal growth. Until victims accept that history can never be rewritten, they may need help in being gently reminded of the reality of the situation – for example, the fact that they are in no way to blame for what happened.

Moving on

Victims have begun to move on when feelings of self-esteem and self-worth return, and they adjust to the new reality and develop a more positive view of the future. Life can never be as it was before the crime, and it is unlikely that the crime will be forgotten. However, memories of the event no longer intrude into everyday life.

Few people are likely to progress smoothly through these stages and most pass to and fro between them. It is important to realise that if, for example, the victim has to go to court, or learns about a similar case from the media, this can take them back to some of their earlier reactions.

While the great majority of victims of crime recover from the trauma of their experience after a few weeks or months, a small number of victims and witnesses of serious crimes cannot move on and become 'stuck' in the recovery process. Others may develop Post Traumatic Stress Disorder (PTSD). A medical condition, diagnosed by a professional doctor or psychiatrist, PTSD is characterised by a cluster of symptoms, some or all of which may be experienced, including violent nightmares, intrusive thoughts of the event or flashbacks, numbing, avoidance and feelings of arousal, confusion and emptiness. Anyone who feels that a victim may be suffering from PTSD should seek professional medical advice.

Regrettably, some victims have their lives changed permanently by crime, for example, because they have been physically injured, scarred or disabled. In addition to their need to come to terms with the other effects of the crime, these victims have to find a new way of living, in which they may be restricted in their ability to do everyday practical things that they used to take for granted. They may also be restricted socially because they fear, or are embarrassed by, other people's reactions to them. This can cause feelings of intense anger or frustration, directed at themselves or other people. What makes it worse is the fact that their injuries were caused by another person's deliberate action, rather than by accident. Learning to live with disablement usually needs professional help and support.

Factors which affect victims' recovery

It is impossible to say how much an individual will be affected by crime or how long it will take them to recover. Generally speaking, the more serious the crime to the victim, the more likely it is to affect them. But there is no automatic link between the apparent severity of the crime and the impact it may have on the victim – victims of burglary can be just as affected as victims of crimes of violence. It is also important not to make assumptions about a victim and their recovery prospects – an elderly woman living alone may recover more quickly, drawing upon her life experiences, than a young man who has a wide group of acquaintances, but no-one in whom he can really confide.

People react to any crisis according to their personality, experience and personal coping resources at the time. These include their state of health, happiness and practical capabilities, as well as their financial means. If they have shown resilience to crises in the past, they may also be able to cope with the effects of crime. In addition, a whole range of influences is likely to affect the way individuals react, from race, social class, gender and culture to the victim's relationship with the offender and their treatment by the criminal justice agencies. Some people who have previously been victims of crime may feel particularly vulnerable in response to further incidents, even if they are unrelated to earlier events. Others will have learned how to cope.

There are a number of other factors that make people particularly vulnerable following a crime and make their recovery more difficult. One of the most significant is the victim's past experience of loss. Such experiences may go back to childhood, and feelings which were not dealt with successfully at the time may be reawakened by the impact of later events. For this reason, children's responses to crime should never be underestimated.

Recent stresses in a victim's personal life may also affect how they respond. These may again be related to loss, for example, through bereavement or divorce, but they may also include problems in marital or family relationships, or at work. If the stresses are so great and the person is suffering, or has suffered, from psychiatric problems, the impact of crime may be all the greater and professional help may be required.

People who lack, or cannot rely on, the support of a close network of family, friends and work colleagues may feel particularly bereft following a crime. A victim's perception at the time of the crime also affects their ability to cope, for example, a relatively minor crime may become more significant in the context of a series of incidents.

The financial effects of crime

The financial effects of crime can be far-reaching. Many crimes happen to people who are already in difficult financial circumstances and any additional expense to repair damage or replace stolen property, or any loss of earnings as a result of injury, can cause serious hardship.

Sometimes goods stolen in a burglary have a high cash value and little sentimental value. More often it is the other way around. But many victims cannot afford household insurance and find it difficult to replace household items. For victims of violence the cost of medical prescriptions or travel to attend hospital or court may also be a burden. And if their reaction to the crime is such that they wish to install state of the art security devices or move home, the associated costs can be significant.

Victims of all crimes may find it impossible to return to work, for a time at least. Not all employers are sympathetic to their requests for leave of absence, with or without pay, to attend hospital appointments or court hearings. Self-employed people may find it difficult to carry on running their business. In such cases, crime can lead victims to lose their livelihood in addition to the other losses that they may have sustained.

Repeat and secondary victimisation

If someone has become a victim of crime, there is a risk of their becoming a victim again. This may be because the crime has occurred because of where they live, for example, because their house is in a vulnerable spot and easy to burgle; or it may be because their lifestyle exposes them to a greater risk. Victims can be helped to develop strategies that will reduce the chance of repeat victimisation, for example, by improving their personal and home security.

Secondary victimisation occurs when people from whom a victim of crime expects to receive understanding fail to respond appropriately. It can make the victim's recovery much more difficult if their family, friends, colleagues or local community fail to be supportive and, for example, try to distance themselves from the crime by either blaming the victim for supposedly putting themselves at risk or urging them to put the crime behind them.

It is also a double injustice to victims, many of whom will have had to summon up a great deal of courage to contact the police, medical services, criminal justice agencies, compensation authorities, and/or insurance companies, if their case is not treated with the respect and seriousness it deserves.

Vulnerable people and crime

Though older people are statistically less likely to become victims of most crimes than younger people, they may feel more vulnerable, especially if they are infirm or cannot hear or see very well. And if they do suffer a crime, its impact may be greater; for example, physical injuries may take longer to heal and emotional scars may stay with them for ever.

Because they spend more time at home, older people are more likely to become victims of doorstep confidence tricksters, who gain admission to their homes by various pretences in order to steal, or who sell products or services at exorbitant cost. Violent callers are rare, but if older people are worried, they may be able to get security devices installed free of charge or at reduced cost as part of a community crime prevention initiative. The police or the local Victim Support or Neighbourhood Watch scheme can provide details.

People with a physical disability, who may not be able to react to danger signals because they cannot see, hear or move away from them, may also feel more anxious about crime. There is no evidence to suggest that they are more likely to become victims, but, like older people, they may be more vulnerable to crimes perpetrated by doorstep confidence tricksters.

To feel more secure at home, it is worth not only taking the usual basic security measures, such as fitting door chains and spy-holes, but also to try to overcome any potential difficulties people may have in summoning help, for example, in getting to a telephone.

People with a learning disability can be particularly unprepared for and shocked by the betrayal of trust that is implied by crime. These problems are intensified if the crime takes the form of physical or sexual abuse in an institution where the offender may be a resident or member of staff.

People with learning disabilities who become victims of crime may have difficulty in telling anyone what has happened and also in describing their experience. If they do tell someone, they may not be believed. In cases that result in prosecution, special measures have recently been introduced to help vulnerable witnesses give evidence in court.

Other people's reactions

The ripple effect of crime

The impact of crime ripples out to affect victims and witnesses, family, friends, neighbours, colleagues and, in some cases, the local and even national community, as well as the professionals who become involved. All these people may experience concern for the victim, fear for the victim's and their own security, and perhaps guilt that they could not, or did not, help.

In addition to the direct victim, other people may therefore suffer as a result of crime. Children as well as parents can be affected by burglary, the friends and family of someone who has been assaulted may also feel threatened and insecure, and the partners of men and women who have been raped may experience extremely strong emotions in response. There is no 'right' way for anyone to cope with crime.

Sparing the grief

Partly because they sense that those closest to them will be disturbed by what has happened, victims may be reluctant to tell family and friends about the crime. In such instances, victims may find it easier to talk to an acquaintance or to someone from Victim Support, who will listen, be supportive and treat everything in confidence and without judgement. Relatives and friends should not be offended by this – by deciding to tell someone else, the victim is beginning to regain control of their life and is taking a step towards recovery.

However, whether they are family, friends, colleagues or strangers, other people should let the victim know that they recognise the seriousness of the crime and are willing to listen if the victim wishes. It is helpful if employers, work colleagues and teachers know about what has happened so that they do not unjustly blame the victim if, as a result of the crime, their behaviour or performance changes or they have to take time off.

Over-protection

Victims may also be reluctant to tell family and friends about their experience because they are frightened that they may respond by blaming them. Especially after a violent or sexual attack, other people may react by taking control, treating the victim like someone who is 'sick'. They may be reluctant to leave them alone and feel they have to accompany them everywhere or make every decision for them. They may also try to protect the victim – and themselves – by avoiding any discussion about violence and censoring newspapers and television programmes.

While it may initially be helpful for victims to feel looked after and protected, in the longer term this may reinforce their feelings of helplessness and prevent them from regaining control. Some victims, for example children, sense that their family may respond by being over-protective and choose not to tell anyone about the crime because they are afraid of losing their independence.

Guilt and anger

Other people may feel guilty if someone they care for becomes a victim of crime because they feel they ought to have been able to protect them. Men may feel guilty by nature of their gender if a partner or daughter is attacked by another man. After a sexual attack a partner may also feel guilty about their feelings towards the victim and afraid to touch them or to express physical affection.

Sometimes family members have even stronger reactions of anger to the crime than the victim. For example, a victim's partner may express particularly violent or vengeful feelings towards the attacker, or channel this towards officials or organisations whom they think could have done more to help. But this may add to the victim's distress, as the victim may feel responsible for what will happen if their partner acts on these feelings.

How you can help

In Victim Support's experience, victims need information, emotional support and practical assistance to help them cope with crime. But before any of these needs can be met, it is important to listen to victims of crime to find out what information, support and assistance is wanted.

Listening to victims of crime can be one of the most useful things a supporter can do. Allowing people to describe their experience in their own words can help them to put it into perspective and begin to regain control of their lives.

Listening may sound easy, but it can be difficult for a listener to stop their thoughts and reactions from getting in the way. Listening also means just that – it does not mean filling up the silences or thinking spaces with time-worn phrases. 'I understand' or 'Time will heal' are meaningless and unhelpful, not only because they minimise the experience and sound condescending, but also because no one can fully understand how another person feels.

Good listeners show empathy, respect and genuineness for the person they are speaking to.

Empathy is the ability to perceive accurately the feelings of another person and to communicate this with warmth. Trying to achieve and demonstrate this involves checking that the listener has interpreted correctly what the speaker has said, and the way they have said it, for example, by noticing their posture, tone of voice and facial expression.

Respect is a frame of mind that involves valuing and accepting someone for what they are. This can mean creating the right setting for a conversation and making sure it is one in which the victim feels safe to talk. It also involves not passing moral judgements on people's behaviour, and valuing their opinions, thoughts and feelings.

The listener shows genuineness by being open with the speaker, not being a 'super supporter', but acting as they genuinely feel at the time and ensuring the victim feels comfortable doing the same. It is also important that the listener is consistent in their verbal and non-verbal behaviour from one meeting to the next.

Showing empathy, respect and genuineness makes it clear that the supporter is in a position to share the victim's thoughts and feelings, accepts them for what they are, and is trying to see things from their point of view.

By listening, the supporter should know whether this is all the victim needs to help them cope with the effects of crime or whether they can do more by providing information, offering practical help and emotional support or putting them in contact with Victim Support.

Ten ways to be a good listener:

  1 provide the victim with the opportunity to talk things over

2 find a comfortable place, where you will not be interrupted, to talk

3 give the victim and the crime your full attention

4 allow the victim to describe their experience in their own words

5 show interest, without interrupting or being impatient to hear the full story or feeling that you have to fill every silence

6 accept what the victim says with respect and without passing judgement

7 watch for unspoken signals about the victim's thoughts and feelings

8 try to see things from the victim's point of view

9 don't adopt the victim's problems as your own

10 be yourself.

Overview

- The police investigation
  - Reporting a crime
  - Police interview and statement
  - Police medical examination
  - Identifying the suspect
  - Follow-up information and support
  - Contacting Victim Support
  - Arresting and charging or cautioning the suspect
  - Bail or remand
- The criminal justice process
  - The Crown Prosecution Service
  - The role of victims and witnesses
  - The Witness Service
  - The protection of vulnerable victims and witnesses
- The prosecution
  - The start of criminal proceedings
  - Summary cases
  - Triable either-way cases
  - Indictable cases
  - The Crown Court Trial
- After the trial
  - Emotional reactions
  - Appeals
  - Custody and supervision
- Other legal options
  - Civil action
  - Private prosecutions
  - Legal help
  - Community Legal Service Fund (formerly Legal Aid)
  - Mediation and restorative justice
- Criminal injuries compensation scheme
  - Background
  - Procedures and eligibility
  - Payment, reviews and appeals
- Standards
  - Charters for court users
  - Victim's Charter

The police investigation

Reporting a crime

The criminal justice process usually starts when a crime is reported to the police. The police investigate the crime to find the offender and the evidence needed to bring the case to court. The investigation will include interviewing the victim and witnesses, taking statements, gathering exhibits and scientific or 'forensic' evidence and obtaining statements from experts who are suitably qualified to give opinions about relevant issues, for example, medical experts who can testify how injuries were caused.

According to the *British Crime Survey*, fewer than 50 per cent of crimes are reported to the police, of which just over half are recorded. And of those crimes which are recorded, not all will be investigated, not least because there may not be evidence for the police to go on. Of those crimes which are recorded and investigated by police, according to the *Recorded Crime Statistics*, around one-third are currently cleared up. The figure varies according to the crime and while only 20 per cent of burglaries are solved, the person responsible is identified in nearly 95 per cent of homicides. However, it is estimated that only two per cent of all crimes that take place result in someone being found guilty of the crime in court.

Police interview and statement

When a crime is investigated by the police, detailed written statements will normally either be taken at the witness's home or at the police station. Victim and witness statements provide the main evidence to support the police investigation and any subsequent prosecution, and it is vital that nothing is concealed or left unclear. Copies of the statements will be made available to the alleged offender's defence lawyers if the matter comes to trial. However, although the statements must record victims' and witnesses' addresses, this information will only be handed over if the victim's address is crucial to the offence, for example, in the case of a burglary. In addition to personal details about their place and date of birth, the police will also ask victims and witnesses whether they have any previous criminal convictions. This is a routine question that the courts may ask about any witness.

Police medical examination

Victims of violent crimes may have to undergo a medical examination by the police doctor. The doctor's report will be used to help the investigation and may be produced as evidence in court. Although the police doctor will provide first aid, the victim may need to consult their own doctor for further treatment.

The police doctor may back up their written report with visual evidence. Photographs of injuries may be taken and the police doctor will also gather what forensic evidence is available from the victim. Victims should therefore not wash or change their clothes before being examined. Their clothing may also be needed as evidence and it is therefore a good idea to take a change of clothing with them to the police station.

Many victims find the examination a distressing experience and it is understandable how their instinct may be to want to wash all traces of the crime away. However, forensic evidence may be vital to the police investigation and if it can be preserved it may help police enquiries.

Identifying the suspect

If the victim or witness can identify the suspect they may need to look at photographs of potential culprits, help a police artist draw a sketch, or attend an identity parade. Less formal identification methods may also be used; for example, the victim may be asked to identify the suspect from a random group of people in a public place. If the victim has not seen the attacker but heard them, voice identification may be tried.

Follow-up information and support

The police should give the victim the name and telephone number of the investigating officer who should tell them if someone is arrested, cautioned or charged with the offence. The officer should in addition keep victims of more serious crimes informed of key stages as the case progresses. The victim may in turn contact the officer if they want to receive or give any more information about the case. This is especially important if they fear or experience further crimes or intimidation. In the most serious crimes, a specific family liaison officer will be appointed to maintain police contact.

In November 1999 the Crown Prosecution Service (CPS) began to pilot an arrangement whereby the prosecutor will, in certain types of case, write to victims to explain decisions to drop or substantially alter the charges. In sexual offences, child abuse and racially aggravated cases, the prosecutor will also offer to meet the victim when charges are dropped or substantially altered.

If the crime results in injury, loss or damage, the police should give the victim a form to complete so that the court has enough information to be able to make a compensation order if the offender is convicted. A compensation order is in addition to any claim the victim may make under the Criminal Injuries Compensation Scheme (CICS) – a state-funded scheme to compensate victims of violent crime (see below). However, the value of any compensation order awarded by the court may be deducted from any award made under the scheme.

The police should also give the victim a 'Victims of Crime' leaflet briefly describing the criminal justice process. This includes information about crime prevention, the Criminal Injuries Compensation Scheme and Victim Support.

Contacting Victim Support

The police should automatically pass the victim's name and address to Victim Support who will then contact them by letter, visit or telephone, to offer its services to help victims cope with their experience. In cases of domestic violence, sexual violence or homicide, the police must ask the victim's permission before referring them to Victim Support. Any victim is entitled to ask for their details not to be passed on.

Victims who are not referred to Victim Support by the police may contact Victim Support directly by contacting the Victim Supportline on 0845 30 30 900 – a national lo-call number. A trained volunteer will then provide help over the telephone and, if the victim wishes, put them in touch with their local scheme.

Arresting and charging or cautioning a suspect

The police have powers to arrest and search a suspect and take possession of their property. They will be interviewed at length and normally have a right to legal advice, but there are restrictions on how long they may be held.

When the police have enough evidence, they must decide whether to charge the suspect or caution them. A caution is a formal warning intended to persuade someone who admits an offence not to reoffend. National guidelines set out the conditions under which a caution may be appropriate. If the offence is too serious for a caution, the police pass the case on to the Crown Prosecution Service (CPS), the agency that is responsible for carrying out most prosecutions. The police are still the main contact for passing information to the victim, but the CPS pilot arrangement referred to above may be extended after evaluation.

Bail or remand

Once charged, the alleged offender must be released on bail, or 'remanded in custody' – that is held in a police station or prison, to appear before the magistrates' court. Both the police and the courts can grant bail. Bail must be granted unless the alleged offender is likely to disappear, reoffend, interfere with or obstruct the course of justice (for example, by threatening witnesses), or if they are already on bail and the offence is serious enough to be tried in the Crown Court.

Conditions may be imposed on the bail, for example, that the alleged offender must appear at the police station at specified times, live at a specific address, or keep away from a location or the victim. Anyone who fails to comply with such conditions can be arrested and bail may be revoked. The court must give reasons for granting bail to someone charged with homicide or serious sexual offences.

When bail is refused and the alleged offender is remanded in custody, the remand must be renewed at a magistrates' court hearing at least every 28 days. If, during one of these hearings, the court grants bail to someone previously held in custody, the court should inform the police and give details of any conditions that are imposed. The police should in turn notify the victim and witnesses.

The criminal justice process

The Crown Prosecution Service

Once the police have completed their investigation and a suspect has been charged, the case papers are passed to the Crown Prosecution Service (CPS). The CPS has a two-stage test to ensure that consistent and fair decisions are made about whether or not to prosecute. According to this, a case will only be continued if there is sufficient evidence to provide a realistic prospect of conviction, and it is decided that prosecution will be in the public interest.

The CPS will, on request, meet the family of someone killed as a result of a crime to explain their decision on prosecution. In other cases, when charges are downgraded or discontinued by the CPS, the police are currently responsible for explaining this to victims. However, as noted above, the CPS is piloting arrangements whereby it will provide the explanation in certain types of case. The Government has said that it intends to transfer this duty to the CPS as soon as resources permit.

The role of victims and witnesses

A description of court procedures follows later in this chapter, but before then it may be helpful to look at what the roles of the victim and the witness are in a prosecution.

In a prosecution the CPS acts on behalf of the general public interest and prosecutes in the name of 'the Crown', not the victim. It can be very hard for victims to understand that they are not a party to the case in the same way that the defence is, and do not have any special rights other than in their role as a prosecution witness who, depending on how the case proceeds, may or may not be called to give evidence. Technically, they should be referred to as the 'alleged victim' unless the defendant is found guilty.

The witness's role

The victim will usually be the main witness for the prosecution but there may also be other witnesses involved in the case. After giving their statement, all witnesses will be contacted by the police to inform them that they may have to attend court to give evidence if the suspect is arrested and prosecuted. They will also be given a contact name to find out more about the case in the meanwhile. At this stage, witnesses should give police details of specific dates when they would not be free to attend a trial, for example because of holidays that have already been booked.

The police are responsible for telling witnesses when they will be needed to give evidence in court. Witnesses do not have to appear for every hearing held in connection with the case – their evidence will be reserved for the trial. When the trial approaches, witnesses are given an early warning that the case may be listed within four weeks. The exact date depends on how long other cases take, and is sometimes only notified to participants the day before.

Witnesses are entitled to claim from the CPS travel expenses for attending court and associated costs, such as childcare and loss of earnings.

The Witness Service

Run by Victim Support, the Witness Service is based in every Crown Court centre in England and Wales. It is currently also being introduced into the magistrates' courts and should be in every criminal court by April 2002. Witness Service staff and volunteers are trained to provide support and information about the court process to witnesses, victims and their families and friends before, during and after the trial.

Before the trial the Witness Service is notified of witnesses who will be called to give evidence and will contact witnesses to offer help if they consent. The Witness Service offers:

- someone to talk to in confidence
- a visit to the court centre beforehand and, where possible, a look around a court room
- information about court procedures
- someone to accompany witnesses into the court room when they give evidence
- practical help, for example with expense forms
- putting people in touch with those who can answer specific questions about the case

● a chance to talk over the case when it has ended and to get more help and advice.

On the day of the trial, victims and witnesses may also be accompanied to the court by their Victim Support volunteer who can offer emotional support to help them cope with their experience. Giving evidence can be very stressful and this is not made easier by the time people may have to wait before they are called into court.

The Witness Service volunteer cannot discuss evidence or offer legal advice but they can help with specific court-based needs, such as arranging for the witness to arrive through a separate entrance where possible, or obtaining a copy of their statement for them to re-read before going into court. Within the courtroom, the Witness Service volunteer must not communicate with the witness in any way, as this may be seen as interfering with the trial.

Despite these rules, being accompanied into court can be helpful because the witness knows that there is at least one person in the room who is supporting them and who can later discuss what happened and what was said.

The protection of vulnerable victims and witnesses

Many witnesses are afraid of giving evidence because they fear reprisals from the offender. However, witness intimidation is itself an offence, and, if witnesses are found to have been intimidated after a trial in which they appeared has resulted in the accused's acquittal, that acquittal may be quashed and a retrial held. Witnesses who are intimidated should tell the police or the CPS immediately and, where necessary, ask for protection.

Special facilities may be available in the court to help witnesses give evidence; for example, interpreters can be arranged for witnesses who do not speak English. Other measures have recently been introduced to protect all vulnerable witnesses. From the end of the year 2000 the Crown Court will be able to consider at the plea and directions hearing (see below) whether some of the measures can be used at the trial. The measures include:

● the use of screens to shield the witness from seeing the defendant

● giving evidence by live closed circuit television link (CCTV)

● presenting evidence on video

● the removal of gowns and wigs by members of the court

● using aids to communication, for example sign boards, to overcome the witness's physical difficulties in understanding or answering questions.

The measures will be available in the magistrates' courts when the necessary resources are found.

The law no longer allows people accused of rape or other sexual offences who represent themselves in court to cross-examine the victim personally. The courts may in some cases extend the same prohibition to other crimes, for example, those involving child witnesses. Restrictions have also been placed on the circumstances in trials for sexual offences in which a victim witness's own sexual history can be discussed.

The media has long been prohibited from identifying victims, witnesses or defendants involved in court cases if they are under the age of 18 or if they are victims of rape or sexual assault. The courts now have the power to extend reporting restrictions to include adult witnesses in other cases, if the court considers it is necessary because of the witness's fear or distress at giving evidence.

The prosecution

The start of criminal proceedings

All criminal proceedings involving adults begin in the magistrates' court, which is usually presided over by three magistrates – lay people – who are advised by a legally qualified clerk. Some courts are run by a single paid or 'stipendiary' magistrate, who is also a lawyer.

Whether cases are concluded in the magistrates' court (97 per cent of all criminal cases are currently concluded here) or passed on to the Crown Court depends on the severity of the case and whether the accused pleads guilty or not guilty. Offences are therefore divided into three categories, according to whether they can be tried in the magistrates' court – 'summary offences' – or are passed on to the Crown Court for trial – 'indictable offences' – or can be tried in either court – 'triable-either-way'.

Although criminal proceedings involving accused children or juveniles under the age of 18 are mostly held in the youth court, all cases of homicide must currently be held in the Crown Court and other serious cases, such as rape and aggravated burglary, may be sent to the Crown Court for trial, depending on the age of the accused and the nature of the offence. Hearings in the youth court are not open to the public.

Summary cases

Summary cases relating to offences such as minor property crimes and assaults begin and end in the magistrates' court. Four out of five people accused of these crimes plead guilty and are sentenced straight away. Where the accused pleads not guilty, the trial is set for a future date.

At that trial, the magistrates will first hear the evidence from the prosecution, including from witnesses, who may be cross-examined by the defence. They will then hear from the defence, who may also call witnesses who may in turn be cross-examined by the prosecution. The magistrates may ask the justice's clerk for legal advice and may or may not adjourn to discuss the case before giving their verdict and passing sentence.

If the defendant is found guilty, the magistrates can sentence them to up to six months' imprisonment and fine them up to £5,000. In certain circumstances they can commit summary offences to the Crown Court for sentencing.

Before sentencing, magistrates may also request a pre-sentence report on the accused from the probation service or the social services department. This may mean a delay or 'adjournment' between conviction and sentence, after which the accused has the right to appeal.

Triable either-way cases

Triable either-way cases may be tried in either the magistrates' court or the Crown Court and relate to offences such as burglary, more serious property crimes and indecent assaults. Where, in view of the nature of the alleged offences, magistrates consider that their sentencing powers will not be adequate, they may choose to send someone who pleads not guilty to the Crown Court for trial. Similarly, where magistrates consider that their sentencing powers are not adequate, they may commit someone who has pleaded guilty to the Crown Court for sentence.

Currently, the accused in such cases also has the right to choose to be tried in the Crown Court. However, this right may be removed if the Government succeeds in its plans to reform the law on the mode of trial in criminal cases.

Indictable cases

Indictable cases relate to crimes that are so serious, for example homicide, rape or robbery, that they must be transferred to the Crown Court, following a preliminary hearing, to be tried before a judge and jury. Witnesses are not required to give evidence at the transfer stage.

The Crown Court trial

The plea and directions hearing

Once a case has been transferred to the Crown Court there will be a 'plea and directions' hearing. If the accused pleads not guilty, the CPS will prepare the case for a full jury trial. This should start within 16 weeks of the case being transferred from the magistrates' court but, in complex cases, such as homicide and rape, this may take up to a year.

Just over half of the defendants who appear in the Crown Court plead guilty, in which case there is no trial and the judge may pass sentence straight away. While it may relieve them of the burden of giving evidence, the lack of a trial can be both frustrating and distressing for victims and victims' families, many of whom will have waited months in anticipation that the full circumstances of the crime may finally be revealed.

If the plea is 'not guilty', it is important that anyone who will be called as a witness leaves the court immediately the plea is taken so that they do not hear the discussion of the future trial. Any witness who fails to leave may jeopardise the trial. The court will then hear the key issues in the case, to ensure that all necessary steps have been taken in preparation for the trial, and to provide the court with any additional information required, including the special needs of witnesses.

The opening of the jury trial

After the plea and directions hearing witnesses will be sent a letter informing them that the trial will soon take place. They will then be told when the date is set. The Witness Service should also receive a list of witnesses summoned to appear and, provided they consent, will contact them with the offer of help.

The trial will be listed in the defendant's name and allocated to a specific court room. There may be a delay before proceedings start, for example, if an earlier case takes longer than expected. All Crown Courts now have a separate waiting area, which reduces the risk of victim and witnesses coming face to face with the accused or their family and friends.

Before the trial opens, the CPS' prosecuting barrister or 'counsel' should introduce themselves briefly to witnesses, but they cannot discuss details of the case. Victims and members of their family and friends, as well as the defendant's family and friends, who are not called to give evidence may sit in the public gallery for the whole of the trial. Witnesses cannot go into the courtroom, including the public gallery, during the trial, before they have given evidence.

The prosecution case

After the jury has been sworn in, the prosecuting counsel acting for the CPS will outline the details of the alleged crime and call their witnesses. Each witness will be questioned by the prosecuting counsel, the 'examination in chief', and then by the defending counsel, the 'cross-examination'. Witnesses may be reexamined on any points raised and the judge may also ask questions. The police officer in charge of the case, together with medical and forensic experts, may also be called to give evidence.

Victims and witnesses may find it traumatic to recollect the circumstances of the crime in detail. They may also feel angry, upset or unnerved if – more probably when – the defence, during cross-examination, casts doubt on what they have said, and appears aggressive or dismissive towards them. Forensic evidence, including photographic material, may also have to be looked at, and in cases of homicide, the pathologist's report will also have to be heard.

The defence case

If the defence believes that the prosecution has failed to present enough evidence for the jury to convict, it may submit that there is 'no case to answer'. The jury will be sent out of the court room while the judge decides. If the judge agrees, the jury will be called back in and directed to acquit the defendant and the case will be closed. If the judge disagrees, the trial will continue.

If the defence wishes to call any witnesses, they will be questioned first by the defence and then by the prosecution. The defendant cannot be compelled to give evidence, but will be the first defence witness to be called if the defence decide to do this. Other defence witnesses may include an alibi witness, character witnesses and experts presenting psychiatric or medical reports.

The defence will try to present a different version of events from that presented by the prosecution. This may add to the victim's feelings that their honesty and reputation are being called into question and that they, not the offender, are being tried. It can leave the victim feeling even more angry if they feel that the circumstances of the crime have been distorted.

Closing speeches and summing up

When all the evidence has been presented, the prosecution and the defence will summarise the case. The judge will then address the jury, highlighting relevant issues on which the case rests and explaining points of law. This may include the fact that they can find the accused guilty of a lesser charge. For example, the jury may find that the accused unlawfully killed the victim but did not intend to commit murder. In these circumstances, the accused could be found guilty of manslaughter.

The verdict

The jury leaves the court to consider its verdict. If they are unable to reach a unanimous verdict they will be called back and the judge will advise them about making a majority decision on which at least ten members agree. If the jury is unable to do this, they will be discharged. Depending on the circumstances, the CPS may apply for a retrial.

The jury must be convinced that the prosecution has proved that the crime has been committed by the accused and that the accused intended to carry it out. The standard of proof is high and the jury must be satisfied 'beyond reasonable doubt' before the accused can be found guilty.

If the verdict is not guilty, and assuming there are no further charges, the accused is freed. Such a verdict does not necessarily mean that the jury believes the accused is innocent, but rather that the defending counsel cast sufficient doubt on the case to make a guilty verdict unsafe. Although the jury may feel great sympathy with the victim, they can only convict on the basis of the evidence. It can be very difficult for the victim to accept this. After all they have suffered, including the ordeal of the trial, they may feel let down and further traumatised. Their emotions and reactions may range from betrayal and anger to disbelief and powerlessness, a sense of injustice and a loss of faith in both the criminal justice system and in society.

Mitigation

If the verdict is guilty, the court will be told about the accused's previous conduct, including convictions. The defence may make a statement in mitigation, putting forward reasons why the sentence should be less severe than it might otherwise be. This may include details of the accused's personal or family circumstances, or it may dispute facts raised by the prosecuting counsel, or even attempt to criticise the victim's character. Judges have the power to restrict reporting by the media of derogatory assertions made by the defence.

Sentencing

Before sentencing, the judge can ask for a pre-sentence report to be prepared, detailing the offence and the circumstances that led up to it. This should include an assessment of how the crime affected the victim, information about the offender, for example previous offending and their likelihood of reoffending, and an assessment of risk to the public.

When sentencing, judges have to take a number of other factors into account in addition to the seriousness of the crime, the circumstances of the offender and any plea in mitigation. These include the effect of the crime on the victim, rehabilitating and deterring the offender or other potential offenders, and demonstrating that the public does not tolerate criminal behaviour. In some cases, the courts must also protect the public by restricting the offender's liberty, whether, for example, by disqualifying them from driving, or sending them to prison.

In the case of murder, life imprisonment is mandatory. Other serious offences, such as rape, manslaughter, robbery and assault inflicting grievous bodily harm, carry a 'discretionary' maximum penalty of up to life imprisonment. However, life imprisonment does not mean that the offender will automatically spend the rest of their life in prison. Most lifers are released on licence after serving part of their sentence, which means they can be recalled to prison if they commit further offences.

The court may suspend a sentence of imprisonment for between one and two years in exceptional circumstances. The sentence will then only be activated if the offender commits another imprisonable offence within that time.

There are generally no limits on the fines that can be ordered in the Crown Court, although these must reflect the seriousness of the offence and take into account the offender's means to pay. Fines are enforced and collected by the magistrates' court.

The court must consider making a compensation order in every case involving death, injury, loss or damage, and give its reasons if a compensation order is not made. Compensation orders can be the only order of the court and should take priority over a fine where the offender has limited means. The orders should acknowledge the victim's pain and suffering, as well as material loss, but, like all financial penalties, awards have to take into consideration the offender's finances and may be reduced or waived altogether if they cannot afford to pay.

The court may also make orders against the offender, for example, regarding community supervision, including probation, or relating to driving disqualification, licence endorsement or to return stolen property or give up drugs or weapons.

An absolute discharge can be given where the offence was extremely trivial or the offender's conduct was only technically an offence. A conditional discharge can be given on the condition that the offender does not commit a further offence during a period of up to three years. If they are convicted of another offence within that time they will be sentenced for the earlier offence as well as the second. Both absolute and conditional discharges are classed as convictions and are listed on the offender's criminal record.

Conviction rates

Victims should be prepared for the fact that the number of crimes that result in a conviction is very few. According to the *British Crime Survey*, only two per cent of offences result in a conviction in either the magistrates' court or the Crown Court.

Cases can fail to reach conviction for a variety of reasons; for example, because the police do not have sufficient evidence to charge a suspect or because the CPS believes the evidence is not strong enough to achieve a conviction or, if the case goes to trial, because the magistrates or the judge and jury are not convinced of the defendant's guilt.

After the trial

Emotional reactions

The emotional impact of the trial on the victim and the victim's family cannot be over-estimated. However, after the many months of waiting and preparation that have led up to it, even a guilty verdict may not bring the sense of release and closure that had been hoped for. A not guilty verdict will be even more distressing and may lead the victim to lose faith in the criminal justice process and in society.

It is therefore after the trial, when the criminal justice authorities are no longer involved in the case, that victims may feel most isolated.

At such times many people turn to Victim Support, whose volunteers offer help regardless of when the crime took place or the outcome of the criminal justice proceedings.

Appeals

The CPS should tell the police if an offender found guilty following a trial decides to appeal, either against their conviction or their sentence. The accused may be allowed bail pending the appeal hearing. In cases of homicide, rape or sexual assault, the police should keep the victim or victim's family informed of the date of the hearing, whether bail is granted, and the result of the appeal.

The prosecution cannot appeal if the accused is acquitted, but it can take steps to try to ensure that an acquittal based on an unfair ruling does not become part of future case law. If the accused is found guilty, victims who are concerned that the sentence is too lenient can write to the Attorney General, as can the CPS or lawyer involved. If the Attorney General agrees, the case may be referred to the Court of Appeal. This must be done within 28 days of the sentence being passed.

Custody and supervision

When offenders are sentenced to four or more years in prison for a serious sexual or violent offence, the probation service should contact the victim or victim's family to explain the custodial process and ask about their concerns regarding the prisoner's eventual release. These anxieties may be taken into account and restrictions might, for example, be placed on where the offender is allowed to work, live or go. The victim or victim's family will not be asked to comment on whether the offender should be released, and they will not be told where the prisoner is being held.

All prisoners serve at least half their sentence in custody. If they are serving more than a year, they will be released between the half-way and two-thirds point, and will be subject to supervision for a period. Some prisoners are allowed short home leave before release.

In addition to the service provided by the probation service, there is a prison service helpline – 0845 758 5112 – for victims of any crime where the offender has been imprisoned. If a victim, for example, receives unwanted contact from a prisoner, or wants to know when they will be released, they can call the helpline and details will be passed to the appropriate prison governor who will respond accordingly.

Other legal options

Civil action

There are occasions where a criminal act can lead to legal action in the civil courts. Typical cases relate to protection when someone wants to obtain a court order or 'injunction' requiring a person to stop doing something. For example, if a man has been accused of domestic violence (see Chapter 5), his partner can apply for an injunction ordering him not to assault her or enter their home. To break an injunction is not a criminal offence, but is treated as 'contempt of court'. The police can only enforce an injunction if it has a 'power to arrest' attached to it.

Professional legal advice should be obtained before beginning any civil action.

Actions may also be brought in which a victim or victim's family brings a civil claim against the offender for injury, property loss or damage. Although a new structure has recently been introduced to try to prevent court fees acting as a barrier to justice, this can still be a lengthy and expensive process and the offender may not have sufficient funds to make suing them financially worthwhile. However, the symbolic value of a judgement, which confirms that the court finds that the defendant did what they are accused of, may be more important to the victim than any financial award.

In addition, suing for damages may be considered if the CPS discontinues a case because it believes the offender's guilt could not be proved 'beyond reasonable doubt'. In civil actions it is only necessary to show 'on the balance of probabilities' that the defendant committed the alleged act. Suing for damages may also be considered if the offender is acquitted on a legal technicality or if the criminal court does not award the victim compensation.

Private prosecutions

In circumstances where the CPS decides not to prosecute a case, it may be possible for a victim of crime, or anyone else, to bring a private prosecution against the alleged offender. In summary cases this must normally be brought within six months of the crime and involves applying to a magistrate to issue a summons. This will usually be granted if the applicant has an arguable case with adequate evidence. The CPS has the right to take the case over at a later date and if it then considers that the prosecution is not in the public interest, the case may be discontinued. This can be extremely distressing for the victim.

Whoever brings the private prosecution can conduct the case themselves, and have a friend to help, but it is important to consider the matter carefully and professional legal advice should be obtained. The consequences of failure can be serious; for example, having to pay the other side's costs, or being sued for damages, if it can be shown that the prosecution was 'malicious'. The case has to be proved 'beyond reasonable doubt' and even if it is won, the accused still has the right to appeal.

Legal help

In civil cases, initial legal advice and assistance may be available to victims under the 'green form scheme', which enables people with limited means in England and Wales to be granted up to two hours of a solicitor's time; Scotland and Northern Ireland have separate schemes.

Victims who are not eligible under the green form scheme may benefit from a fixed fee interview. Solicitors should be asked in advance if they offer this service and what the fee is for an assessment of the victim's legal position. In some areas, law centres give free legal advice. Although not legally qualified themselves, organisations such as Victim Support and the Citizens Advice Bureau may be able to put victims in touch with people who can help.

Community Legal Service Fund (Legal Aid)

People with limited means have previously been entitled to apply for Legal Aid to fund the costs of legal advice and taking action in the civil courts, for example, to sue an offender for compensation or to seek an injunction to protect them from a violent partner.

The Legal Aid Board, which adminsters the Legal Aid Fund, is in the process of being replaced by the Legal Services Commission. The new agency will run two new funding schemes, the Community Legal Service for family and civil cases, and the Criminal Defence Service for criminal cases. As previously, financial eligibility limits will be set for people to receive services funded by the schemes. It is expected that these will initially be similar to those set for Legal Aid, but it is hoped to expand the scheme to areas that are not currently covered, for example, to extend access to mediation services.

Mediation and restorative justice

Where a crime occurs because of a dispute between people who are known to one another, for example between neighbours, a criminal prosecution or civil action is not the only option.

In some areas of the country, there are community mediation services, which can offer help in cases like this. A hearing is arranged, led by mediators, who are trained volunteers, which allows both parties to give their account of what happened in their own words. The mediator then helps the parties to understand more about each other's stance and find both common ground and a solution to their conflict, without attempting to decide who was to blame. The service is free and confidential, and no-one's legal rights are affected if an agreement is not reached or kept.

The Crime and Disorder Act 1998 brought the principle of mediation or 'restorative justice' into the mainstream criminal justice system for the treatment of young offenders. Some police forces and probation services have also adopted a mediation approach and independently pioneered supervised meetings between victims and offenders of all ages, and at almost any stage of the criminal justice process.

The aim of restorative justice is to help repair the damage done by crime by arranging for victim–offender meetings or including reparation to the victim, for example making a personal apology, as part of a sentence. Such meetings allow the victim to explain how the crime has affected them and to question offenders about the crime. In turn, they allow the offender to appreciate the consequence of their actions and make up for, and learn from, the suffering they have caused. Victims do not have to take part in such meetings, but those who do may find that it helps to reduce their fears, for example of revictimisation by the same offender.

Criminal injuries compensation scheme

Background

State compensation for injuries caused to victims of violent crime, which was introduced in the UK in 1964, is handled by the Criminal Injuries Compensation Authority (CICA). The scheme was revised in 1995 and a fixed scale or 'tariff' of payments was established for specific injuries. Under the tariff, the current minimum amount payable is £1,000 and the maximum is £250,000. For example, someone who has sprained an ankle as a result of a violent crime may be awarded £1,000, but someone who is left paralysed in all four limbs may be awarded £250,000.

Victims of crime can apply for state compensation themselves and do not need to be legally represented. However, in order to cover the many circumstances that can arise, the rules are lengthy and many victims find it helpful to seek advice from a solicitor, Law Centre or from the Citizens Advice Bureau. Victim Support helps victims of all crimes to deal with thousands of compensation claims every year, but it cannot offer legal advice. The brief notes that are given here are based on the CICA's guidelines.

Victims who seek legal advice cannot claim the cost of that advice from the CICA, although some victims may be entitled to receive a free initial legal consultation under the green form scheme (see above). Criminal injuries compensation application forms are available from the CICA, police stations, Victim Support schemes and Citizens Advice Bureaux.

Procedures and eligibility

Claims for state-funded compensation may be made either for personal injury by the direct victim of a violent crime or, in cases that result in the victim's death, for fatal injury by the direct victim's parents, children or partner. A former husband or wife who was financially supported by the deceased may also submit a fatal injury claim. In fatal cases, an application may also be considered for reimbursement of reasonable funeral expenses.

Applications for children under the age of 18 should be made by parents, or an adult or local authority with legal responsibility for the child.

Claimants for state compensation have to be:

- a victim of a crime of violence or injured in some other way covered by the scheme
- physically and/or mentally impaired as a result
- living in or visiting England, Scotland or Wales at the time when the injury was sustained (Northern Ireland, Jersey, and the Isle of Man have their own schemes); and
- injured seriously enough to qualify for at least the minimum award available; or
- a dependant or relative of the victim of a crime of violence who has since died.

As soon as a claim has been received, the CICA will acknowledge the application and allocate a personal reference number that should be used for further enquiries. The authority will then make enquiries of the police, medical authorities and other bodies to enable the claim to be assessed.

Each application is considered individually and decisions are made according to published guidelines. Claims are determined by the authority's officers who will first decide whether the application fits the scheme's basic criteria and whether it may be witheld or reduced on account of other factors. These factors include whether the victim or claimant has a criminal conviction; whether the victim's conduct before, during or after the incident makes it 'inappropriate' that they should receive an award, for example whether they in any way provoked the attack. Unless there are good reasons, claimants should in addition have reported the incident to the police as soon as possible after it happened, and cooperated with the police in bringing the offender to justice. Completed application forms should be submitted within two years of the crime.

Reasons will be given in cases where awards are witheld or reduced. Claimants should try to prepare themselves for the distress this can cause, for example, if they are told that their application has been rejected because it did not fit the criteria. While this may be technically correct, such statements do little to help the victim come to terms with the crime. Talking to someone from Victim Support may be especially helpful at such a time.

Payment, reviews and appeals

Compensation awards that are granted may be made in full by a single payment, or as an interim award, pending further consideration. The CICA may reconsider its decision to make a final award any time before it is paid.

If a person is receiving means-tested state benefits, for example income support, the Department of Social Security counts the award as 'capital', and the victim's benefit may be reduced. This can be avoided by using the award to purchase an annuity, through an insurance company, which will then provide a regular annual income, or by putting the money into a trust fund, which will similarly provide regular payments. However, the income from an annuity or trust may still count against benefits and it is important to seek professional advice before deciding what to do.

Claimants who are not satisfied with the CICA's decision can write to the authority giving reasons and requesting a review. This must be done within 90 days of the date of the original decision. The review will be carried out by a senior officer and a fresh decision will be made. Claimants who are still not satisfied can appeal to the Criminal Injuries Compensation Appeals Panel. The appeal must be lodged within 30 days of the date of the review decision.

Standards

Charters for court users

Crown Courts have been set standards of performance, listed in the Courts' Charter, which should be on display in every court building. These set specific targets, for example, for the time it should take for cases to come to court.

Magistrates' courts also have a model quality of service charter, which similarly includes service standards, for example on waiting times and meeting the needs of disabled court users.

Anyone who feels that these standards are not met can contact the court manager, who should then investigate and reply with their findings.

Victim's Charter

Other organisations working in the criminal justice sector have also been set standards of performance relating to their work with victims and witnesses of crime in the Victim's Charter. These include the police, the Crown Prosecution Service, probation service, the Criminal Injuries Compensation Authority, Victim Support and the Witness Service run by Victim Support.

Overview

Homicide

The crime figures provide no measure of the number of people affected by homicide. Those immediately bereaved in the family – mothers, fathers, wives, husbands, partners, children, brothers, sisters, grandparents – have their lives disrupted. Friends, neighbours, work colleagues will all suffer too.

People bereaved by homicide find that the assumptions they held about themselves and their world are shattered. A malevolent human act has taken away the person they loved. Grief is always a powerful emotion, but after homicide it may be accompanied by extreme anger, depression, anxiety and fear. Some people will be so severely affected that they develop a serious condition known as Post Traumatic Stress Disorder (PTSD).

The pain and chaos are worsened by the fact that other people simply do not understand – how can they? Yet it is important to try. What is known about the effects of bereavement by homicide indicates that, as in other situations of extreme distress, the reactions of others may do much to help or hinder recovery. This is particularly important in situations where family members may no longer be able to help one another – because of what has happened.

Bereaved people reading this, and those who are trying to help them, will know that life can never be the same again. The anniversaries of the death, the birthday of the loved one, are powerful annual landmarks. After homicide, the criminal justice system brings further landmarks: the date of the trial (most perpetrators of homicide are brought to justice) and the progression of the sentence. The aim of this chapter is to foster understanding and to encourage those affected to seek help.

In the midst of their shock and confusion, homicide precipitates people into the strange world of the law. A senior police officer will be put in charge of the investigation. A specially trained family liaison officer will also be appointed to ensure that the family is provided with appropriate information throughout the investigation. The police are also responsible for providing the family with a special Home Office information pack containing details about the criminal justice system, grief reactions, and the help that is available.

The family liaison officer will normally discuss with the family whether they wish to be put in touch with Victim Support. Victim Support has volunteers who are specially trained to help families bereaved by homicide to cope with the impact of such a horrific crime. The Victim Supportline on lo-call number 0845 30 30 900 can also put people directly in touch with someone who can help.

Other organisations, such as Support After Murder and Manslaughter (SAMM), also offer specialised support in such circumstances. A self-help group whose members find that helping others gives a sense of purpose to their own lives, SAMM has particular expertise in supporting the parents of murdered children, but offers its help to the family and friends of all murder and manslaughter victims.

How people react to homicide

General responses to bereavement

Common reactions to any bereavement include grief, shock, numbness, bewilderment, disbelief, guilt, panic, depression, anger and irritability. People may be absent-minded or restless, unable to sleep or eat properly, and may cry uncontrollably. They may dream of the deceased and want to carry reminders of them. These responses are part of the natural grieving process, some or all of which may be experienced in overlapping phases over time. However disturbing, these usually give way to the bereaved person accepting their loss, adjusting to the new reality, and re-entering the everyday world.

Bereavement through homicide

What is different for people bereaved through homicide is that death has been sudden and deliberate, with no preparation or chance for them to say goodbye. The killing of another human being is the most violent action there is and families and friends are thrown into an emotional turmoil for which nothing can prepare them. If the murder has been committed by someone they know, if they have witnessed the act, or if the person who died has not been found, their feelings are still more complicated.

In such circumstances, normal grief reactions may be more intense, last longer, or become distorted and lead to traumatic grief. People may re-experience the death through dreams and flashbacks. They may feel hatred towards the perpetrator and experience strong, macabre desires for revenge, which may make them frightened or ashamed. They may feel they cannot confide in anyone and become withdrawn and depressed. The duration and intensity of such anger may mask or delay other grief reactions.

Living in fear

It is easy to understand how such conflict adds to the stress of bereavement and can lead someone to fear that they are 'going mad'. But people may also fear that the perpetrator will come back and attack them or harm other family members. This may be either a general sense of unease or a well-founded sense of danger. All security fears should be discussed with the police.

People bereaved by homicide may especially feel that their belief in a 'safe world' has been shattered and as a result become over-protective, particularly of children. In some cases, the fear may lead to phobias that prevent the bereaved person leading a normal life.

Guilt and blame

Feelings of guilt and blame are among the most difficult for bereaved people to cope with. People may go back over the events that led up to someone's death and blame themselves or someone else for not preventing it. Such feelings, particularly if the person blames a partner or other family member, may be difficult to acknowledge and work through. They may also create rifts, which prevent people from supporting those close to them.

People may blame society for allowing the crime to be committed. They may feel wounded a second time; for example, if they feel that the police are not doing everything they can to apprehend the killer or if the accused is found not guilty of the crime. More complex feelings can occur if society 'stigmatises' the victim or their family and suggests that they were in some way responsible for their death. This can be the case, for example, if the victim had a criminal record. In such cases the media or the criminal justice system, may draw attention to details of their lifestyle, implying that they made themselves vulnerable to attack. In cases where a child is killed, it may be the parents whose lifestyle is subject to scrutiny.

Different responses to grief

Children bereaved by homicide suffer intense grief and even more so if they have witnessed the killing. In addition to the above symptoms, they may be easily startled, suffer from nightmares or digestive upsets and cut themselves off from their family and friends.

Grieving is especially difficult for them and if they are not helped it may limit their ability to trust people and make new attachments in the future. Victim Support volunteers can help parents and carers to help their children to come to terms with their experience.

Adults also have different ways of experiencing and demonstrating grief. Some put all their energies into specific practical tasks or want to take an active part in an organisation that helps victims of similar crimes. Others cannot do anything other than focus on their own grief and the person who has been killed. All are doing what is right for them – no-one should feel that they are over-reacting or under-reacting to their tragedy.

In some people, the emotional turmoil of sudden bereavement will manifest itself in physical illness. Symptoms may be as varied as panic attacks, headaches, skin rashes, muscle tension and difficulty in swallowing. In spite of everything, the bereaved person needs to look after their health and keep as close as possible to their normal routine.

Social effects

Some bereaved people may join in social activities but just play the part of having a good time. Others become isolated from friends or their communities, perhaps because they or their friends find it difficult to talk about the death or cannot cope with what has happened or are acting differently as a result. In such circumstances friendships may end and even intimate relationships may be undermined, leading to break-up. People may also feel society has withdrawn from them – some describe how other people seem to go out of their way to avoid them as if they are frightened of homicide as of catching a disease.

Most employers understand that someone bereaved by homicide will not be able to return to work for some time – usually at least a month. However, when the person does return, there may be difficulties in communicating with colleagues who may need to be guided in whether or not they wish to talk about what has happened. There is a need for understanding on both sides.

Financial effects

Financial matters can be very difficult for people bereaved through sudden death, particularly if the victim contributed to the family budget. For example, access to the victim's bank accounts may not be possible until the death certificate has been issued and in the meanwhile there may be many expenses to meet in addition to the funeral. These may include, for example, the cost of cleaning the house if the crime happened there, but later on there may be additional hidden costs, such as the reduction in the value of a property where a murder has taken place. Income may be reduced, not only because the family was financially dependent on the victim, but also because other members of the family may feel unable to return to work temporarily or even permanently as a result of the crime.

Even if life assurance policies are in place, it may take time to resolve a claim. There are no specific state benefits to help people bereaved through homicide and no additional statutory social rights, for example to housing or medical care, but crisis loans may be available in some cases – the local benefits agency will advise. After a homicide, close family members can claim an award from the Criminal Injuries Compensation Authority, but this may also take months to be assessed and granted (see Chapter 2).

What happens after homicide

The scene of the crime

When a suspicious death is discovered, the police will seal off the area, check the identities of everyone present and guard the victim's body until a doctor arrives to confirm the death and the body is then taken to the mortuary. The investigating officer will establish a major incident enquiry and assign the tasks of gathering evidence.

If the crime takes place at the victim's home, the police may arrange temporary accommodation for other residents until the search for evidence is completed. If the victim has been killed elsewhere, relatives may wish to visit the scene of the crime. In such cases, the police will usually provide them with the information they need to do so.

Breaking the news

If the victim's death is not already known to the family, because a family member has witnessed the killing or discovered the body, the police will inform the victim's next of kin of the death. The family may then wish to contact other relatives and friends before they learn of the death from somebody else or from the media. Care obviously needs to be taken to ensure that the information is presented gently, but not telling people the truth, including children, may leave them with too many unanswered questions and affect their ability to grieve.

The role of the coroner

It is the coroner's duty to find out the medical cause of death if it is not known, or if it was due to violence or was otherwise sudden, unexpected or unnatural. An experienced doctor or lawyer, the coroner is an independent judicial officer whose responsibilities include arranging for a post-mortem examination and an inquest into deaths reported to them. The coroner has to keep all documents relating to the case for 15 years. They can be seen, without charge, by anyone with a legitimate interest in the case.

Identification of the body

The police will make arrangements for a family member to identify the victim's body at the mortuary. Arrangements to view the body other than for formal identification should be made through the coroner's office. The coroner's office will also tell the family when and where the inquest will be held, when the death certificate will be issued and what funeral arrangements may be made.

Some mortuaries discourage private visits and prefer families to wait until the body is taken to the funeral director's. However, people may want to say goodbye to the deceased before then and they are usually allowed to do so. Whatever the circumstances, people need to be prepared – for the clinical surroundings of the mortuary and the extent of the victim's injuries.

The post-mortem

The coroner will arrange for a post-mortem examination to be carried out by a pathologist to determine the cause of death. No charge against a defendant can be made until this is established. The family may be represented at the post-mortem by their doctor. They are also entitled to inspect the examination report, to purchase a copy or request that a copy is sent to their doctor.

If the family is unhappy with the findings of the first examination, the coroner may permit an additional post-mortem at their expense. If someone is later charged with the offence, they also have a right to a second post-mortem. However, guidelines have recently been issued to the police and to coroners to try to ensure delays are kept to the minimum and that the victim's body will be released to the family where possible within 28 days of the discovery of the offence. In some cases, the coroner will release the body for burial only.

The inquest

An initial inquest will be held to establish the victim's identity, and when, where, and how they died. The inquest will then be adjourned while the criminal investigation proceeds.

If someone is prosecuted for the offence, a second hearing will take place after the trial to close the inquest formally. If no prosecution is brought, the coroner will arrange for a full inquest hearing to establish the full facts of the death and decide a verdict of either accidental death, death by misadventure, unlawful killing or an open verdict. A jury may be appointed to determine the cause of death according to the evidence, which is sworn on oath. The family is entitled to ask questions at the inquest or to instruct a solicitor to do so on their behalf. They may also ask for witnesses to be called. However, an inquest is not a trial and it does not apportion blame or settle liability, although the coroner may make recommendations to prevent similar fatalities in the future. The coroner will then close the inquest formally.

Relatives need to be prepared for the fact that inquests are held in public and may be reported in the media, and that during the inquest the death may be discussed in great detail and photographic evidence may be shown.

The victim's death has to be preliminarily notified to the registrar of deaths within five days of the initial inquest being adjourned. The registrar will issue the final death certificate within 28 days of the inquest being formally closed. Death certificates are important documents and problems can be caused if they cannot be issued until the inquest is closed. For example, families may not be able to access the victim's bank account and this can lead to them suffering financial hardship in addition to all their other distress.

The unsolved case

The majority of homicides are solved by the police, but in cases where all avenues of enquiry have been followed up and no-one has been charged, the scale of the investigation is eventually reduced. Such cases are 'left open' and if further information becomes available, they may be investigated actively again and the family informed.

Cases which do not go to trial

In cases where the Crown Prosecution Service (CPS) decides there is insufficient evidence to prosecute and charges against the defendant are dropped, the family is entitled to ask the CPS for an interview to explain their decision. Some families may wish to consider bringing a private prosecution, but this must be done within six months of the crime and professional legal advice is essential.

Cases which do go to trial

All criminal cases begin in the magistrates' court (see Chapter 2). Homicide cases are subsequently committed to the Crown Court for trial.

In some cases, the victim's friends and relatives who are not called as witnesses and are therefore not obliged to attend the trial, may find the experience of doing so too distressing. However, in order to try to understand the circumstances of the victim's death and to try to bring some kind of closure to the tragedy, they may still wish to know the details of the proceedings. In the past, the cost of obtaining a written transcript of the trial has been prohibitive, but proceedings in many Crown Courts are now taped and families may therefore be able to obtain a record in this cheaper format.

Families who do wish to attend the trial may find it easier to cope with the experience with the help of a volunteer from Victim Support's Witness Service (see Chapter 2).

For murder, the only sentence that a judge can hand out is life imprisonment. For manslaughter, the sentence is up to life imprisonment. Most life sentence prisoners may be released after a number of years, but there are restrictions and they can be recalled to prison. The victim's family will be asked whether they wish to be informed when a prisoner serving a sentence for murder or manslaughter is being considered for home leave or parole.

Compensation

The parents, partners and children of homicide victims are entitled to claim state compensation from the Criminal Injuries Compensation Authority (CICA) for their loss (see Chapter 2). In some cases, the CICA may also grant awards to cover the cost of funeral expenses and the cost of providing a tombstone.

Dealing with the media

The families of homicide victims may face a barrage of media enquiries immediately following the crime. This is partly because restrictions limiting what can be reported only come into force when someone is charged. After that everyone – the family as well as the media – must be careful about what they say, in order not to prejudice the trial. The police and Victim Support can help families to deal with media enquiries.

Not all contact with the media is negative. During the investigation the police may hold a press conference to appeal for witnesses or for further information. The family may be asked to select a photograph of the victim, which will be copied and given to the media, and a family member may be asked to attend the conference. The media may also help the family come to terms with the victim's death by allowing them to tell their story and pay tribute to the victim's life or, after the trial is over, help them campaign to try to prevent similar crimes.

Simple ways to help

Many people want to help relatives and friends bereaved by sudden death but do not know how. The value of simply being there cannot be over-estimated but, with their permission, many other tasks can also be carried out on their behalf.

Above all it's important for other friends and relatives to keep in touch with those closest to the victim. If you don't know what to say, say just that, rather than avoiding the family through embarrassment, or recycling phrases such as 'Time will heal', 'You'll get over it', or 'I understand'. Listening, showing comfort and compassion, and allowing people to express their emotions may be more useful than talking (see Chapter 1).

It is especially important to take care of people at such a time. After the shock of a sudden death, people may find it difficult to concentrate, eat, drink or sleep – simple shopping, cooking, cleaning, driving people about, or even looking after a pet, can be a tremendous help.

Helping to inform other people who need to be told of the death can also be of use, for example employers and schools, distant relatives and friends, banks and building societies, benefits agencies and tax offices, hire purchase, insurance and credit card companies.

Many people bereaved by homicide will also need help to cope with the necessary official procedures and arrangements that are involved, for example the identification of the body and the inquest. Enquiries will also have to be made about when funeral plans can be made, and when property will be returned from the police.

These are distressing tasks for anyone to undertake and it may be helpful to seek support from Victim Support. Victim Support volunteers are specially trained to help bereaved families and their friends and relatives to cope in such circumstances. Interviews with people who have received assistance from Victim Support indicate that it is more effective to receive help early. In this way, the volunteer is able to receive the full range and intensity of the emotions and reactions the family experiences and is therefore in a better position to help them cope with the full impact of the crime.

Sexual Violence

4

Overview

- Sexual violence
- How people react to sexual violence
  - Victims' reactions
  - Male victims' reactions
  - Responsibility for the crime
  - Reactions of partners, family and friends
  - Social effects
  - Financial effects
  - Longer-term effects
- What happens after sexual violence
  - Reporting the crime
  - Police involvement
  - Seeking medical help
  - HIV/AIDS
  - The criminal justice process
  - Downgrading of charges and discontinuance of cases
  - Court and sentencing procedures
  - Media attention
- Simple ways to help

Sexual violence

The legal definition of crimes of sexual violence describes in clinical terms some of the most emotionally damaging crimes victims can suffer. For this reason, it may be weeks, months or even years before they can begin to acknowledge and talk about their experience.

Committed against men and women of all ages, crimes such as rape, attempted rape, buggery and indecent assault are expressions of violence and are usually motivated not by sexual desire but by the offender's desire for power and control.

The impact such crimes may have on their victims cannot be over-estimated, although it is often difficult for partners, family and friends to understand. By reading this, it is hoped that they will be more aware of what the victim is going through and how they might be able to help, including telling them about Victim Support.

Victim Support has volunteers who are specifically trained to help victims cope with the effects of sexual violence and who will talk to them free of charge, in complete confidence. Victims who report crimes of sexual violence to the police should be asked whether they wish to be referred to Victim Support. People who do not report the crime may contact Victim Support directly, either by contacting their local Victim Support scheme whose telephone number is in the local directory, or by telephoning the Victim Supportline on lo-call number 0845 30 30 900.

How people react to sexual violence

Victims' reactions

The general effects of crime described in Chapter 1 can be experienced with intensity by victims of sexual violence. People describe feeling frightened, guilty, powerless, angry, ashamed and depressed, and having difficulty eating, sleeping or concentrating. Many victims feel that they have lost control over their lives and that their self-esteem has been undermined. If their partner is the offender, the impact may be even greater. The victim's ability to cope with the trauma may also be affected by the real or imagined reactions of partners, family and friends.

Male victims' reactions

Most of the information in this chapter applies equally to male and female victims of sexual violence. Many victims delay seeking help, or talking about their experiences, and suffer embarrassment, shame or guilt. But men may feel additionally that their victimisation is an affront to their masculinity. This can be made worse if people ask them why they did not resist more strongly.

If their attackers were male, the victim may be confused and wonder whether he gave them homosexual 'vibes', especially if he experienced sexual arousal during the attack. Yet arousal in such circumstances can be a physical response provoked by fear. The victim may have problems with relationships as a result of the crime, and feel revulsion to the point of sexual phobia, or fear that he has a sexually transmitted disease, especially AIDS, or develop sexual apathy or impotency. They may also be concerned about the reactions of the police if they report the crime.

Male sexual violence is motivated more by anger and aggression than by sexual desire. Some attacks on men may be homophobic, but such crimes are not primarily gay crimes and many assailants and victims are heterosexual.

Responsibility for the crime

There is a tendency for society to speculate whether victims of sexual violence were partly responsible for the crime. Attention may be drawn in the media, or even in court, to details of the victim's appearance or lifestyle that supposedly made them vulnerable. This only serves to diminish the victim's trauma and excuse their attacker's actions, thereby protecting society's belief that nothing untoward happens to people unless they deserve it. Whatever the circumstances of the crime, someone else – not the victim – is to blame.

Reactions of partners, family and friends

A victim's reluctance to discuss the crime with friends, family or even partners may result from the fear of being judged or the desire to protect loved ones' feelings. People should not feel hurt if a victim prefers to talk to someone else.

When a crisis for one family member rebounds on others, they must be allowed to react in their own way. Common reactions to sexual violence include anger, guilt, denial, being over-protective, and openly or privately blaming the victim. Partners' anxieties need particularly to be addressed. They may wonder whether the victim resisted their attacker, or they may want to be supportive but feel they have no right to intrude on the victim's pain. Sexual relationships may be damaged by unspoken feelings and fears on both sides. If problems persist, the victim and their partner may benefit from therapy.

Children may be especially affected by sexual violence against a parent who may be suddenly unable to meet their day-to-day needs. They may be disturbed by seeing their parent(s) distressed and respond with uncharacteristic or regressive behaviour, for example bedwetting, sleeplessness and becoming demanding or aggressive. Health visitors or their school's educational psychological service can often help.

Parents have to decide whether, or what, to tell children about the crime. It is likely that children will already be aware that something has happened, even if they do not know what. They may even fear that they are in some way responsible. Sexual violence may also take place in the wider context of domestic violence that children have already witnessed (see Chapter 5).

Telling children what has happened may make them frightened of a world in which such things can happen, but they may be even more confused by overhearing a distorted version of events from someone else than if they are told clearly and calmly by their parents and allowed to ask questions. Nevertheless, only the victim can decide whether to tell their children and what details to discuss.

Social effects

The experience of sexual violence may for a time affect a victim's ability to live their daily life and relate to family, friends and society as a whole. Some people do not feel able to go to work, because they cannot concentrate or cannot face people. Others feel unable to be on their own or, if the attack took place at home, cannot face going home at all. They may even want to move house, especially if the offender lives nearby. If the victim's home is rented from a housing association or local council it may be possible to apply for a housing transfer.

Financial effects

Sexual violence can also create financial problems. If a victim has to take time off work they may lose income and, unless they have an understanding employer, even lose their job. There will also be additional expenses to meet. The victim may need to go away for a while to try to recover, or replace clothes they were wearing at the time, or redecorate their home and make it more secure. If they feel they have to move house, the additional costs are substantial, and if a baby is born as a result of the attack, the long-term costs of looking after the child are only partly met by social security.

Successful claims to the Criminal Injuries Compensation Authority (CICA) may help victims to meet some of these costs (see Chapter 2). However, it can take months or even years before claims are granted and paid. There is also the possibility that claims will be rejected because the claim does not meet all of the CICA's criteria.

Longer term effects

Some victims of sexual assault will be seriously affected in the longer term. The effects can be physical, mental or emotional, and serious depression or Post Traumatic Stress Disorder (PTSD) may result. A medical condition, diagnosed by a professional doctor or psychiatrist, PTSD is characterised by a cluster of symptoms, some or all of which may be experienced, including violent nightmares, intrusive thoughts of the event or flashbacks, numbing, avoidance and feelings of arousal, confusion and emptiness. Victims who may be suffering from PTSD should seek professional medical advice.

It is unhelpful for victims of sexual violence to be told they will 'get over it'. Victim Support can help by providing someone to listen to and take the victim's feelings at face value, even long after the crime. The support of a sympathetic GP is invaluable and, depending on the victim's situation, they may refer them to a specialist service, for example to a professional counsellor or trauma clinic.

What happens after sexual violence

Immediately after the attack the victim's safety and health must come first. In some cases, the police and/or ambulance service will have been called, by the victim or someone else. It is important that the victim is given every opportunity to tell a caring, responsible person whether they know their attacker and/or have any fear of further attack.

It may be important to give attention to safety, without making any assumptions about later police involvement. Someone who has been sexually assaulted may require emergency treatment for their injuries.

Reporting the crime

The victim must decide whether or not to report the crime to the police. This is especially difficult if their attacker is a partner or an acquaintance.

Reasons given by some people for not reporting the crime include shame or guilt that they have been attacked sexually, however mistaken such feelings may be. They may also include fear of an unsympathetic response from the police and from people they know, or of retaliation by the offender. Victims may also be concerned about the ordeal of the legal process, after which the offender may still be found not guilty.

It may help to know that police forces in the UK have devoted a great deal of effort in recent years to special training to support the service they offer to victims of sexual violence. Officers who deal with victims will try to balance the needs of the investigation with awareness of the victim's experience, although it will never be easy, either for the victim to make a statement about what has happened or to undergo a medical examination for the purposes of providing forensic evidence.

Some victims find that reporting the crime helps them to take control over what has happened and helps their emotional recovery. Others feel that reporting the crime may help to protect other people from similar attacks.

Victims may report crimes to the police either by phone or in person. However, at some point, victims of sexual violence will usually have to go to the police station, for example, in order to be examined by the police doctor, and they may feel better if someone accompanies them.

Police involvement

Some police forces have introduced special rape suites for interviewing victims of sexual violence. These are designed so that the victim can be questioned and then medically examined by a specially trained police doctor in a less intimidating atmosphere.

Some victims find that it helps if they are accompanied to the police station by a friend, family member, or Victim Support volunteer.

Others may prefer to deal with the police officer and doctor themselves, but to know that support is available afterwards. Most people are aware that early forensic evidence may be vital in an investigation and some victims are able to respond to police requests to provide it. However, feelings of being sullied and dirty are common after sexual attack so it is important that victims who have showered or changed their clothes should not be blamed for this. Some police facilities for victims of sexual assault are able to provide a shower and clean clothes before the victim goes home.

A police doctor will carry out the medical examination. They may also take photographs of external injuries and use outline body drawings to record internal injuries. Some victims of sexual violence have strong feelings about whether they would prefer to see a male or female doctor and police officer. Police procedures recognise this, and it is often possible, for example, for a woman who has been raped to see a female officer. Victims are also entitled to expect, however, that all officers involved in the investigation deal with them sensitively. The availability of women doctors is better in some areas than others and cannot always be guaranteed.

The victim's statement to the police is likely to be the main evidence in any court case. It is important that everything is noted correctly and fully. Statements are sometimes taken in two parts – a preliminary interview followed by a detailed statement later.

If the victim does not report an attack straight away, they can still do so later – many victims wait for months, even years, before talking about sexual violence. The need to talk may be triggered by similar violence to themselves or someone they know, or by something they read about or witness in real life or through the media.

Victims of any form of violence can apply for state-funded compensation through the Criminal Injuries Compensation Scheme. Delay in reporting may affect any compensation claim made, but a claim is not automatically refused if a crime is not reported promptly. Compensation awards may also be made in relation to crimes that are reported but not taken to court (see Chapter 2).

Seeking medical help

Whether or not victims of sexual violence report the crime, they should seek medical treatment. Injuries are best treated quickly at a hospital accident and emergency department. Both male and female victims are entitled to ask to see a woman doctor. Medical staff should treat the victim on a confidential basis and not report the incident to the police, unless the patient requests this.

It may be hard for the victim to think about other health issues but tests for sexually transmitted diseases are important, even if the victim shows no signs of ill health. In addition, some women may be concerned that they may have become pregnant as a result of the attack and will want to have a pregnancy test.

Most sexually transmitted diseases are easily cured if detected early enough and some victims find that arranging for these tests helps the recovery process. Many victims are left feeling dirty after sexual violence and thinking that they might have an infection reinforces this. Knowing what is going on in their body and taking action or starting treatment may help.

Family planning centres and GPs offer free and confidential pregnancy testing, 'morning after' contraception, and help with making decisions about a pregnancy. Tests for sexually transmitted diseases can be carried out at the genito-urinary medicine clinic of any hospital – it need not be the victim's local hospital – and people do not have to be referred by their GP.

HIV/AIDS

The Human Immunodeficiency Virus (HIV) is the sexually transmitted disease that causes most victims of sexual offences the greatest concern. HIV can be transmitted through unprotected anal and vaginal sex and from one person's blood to another's. HIV is a virus that can damage the body's defence system so that it cannot fight off certain infections. If someone with HIV goes on to get certain serious illnesses, the condition is known as Acquired Immune Deficiency Syndrome (AIDS). There is no cure for HIV or for AIDS, but there are treatments that delay the onset of AIDS and there are cures and treatments for many of the illnesses that people with HIV are prone to. Not everyone who contracts HIV goes on to develop AIDS.

Anyone who feels that they may have been at risk should contact a genito-urinary medicine clinic to discuss being tested. The test is a simple blood test but the virus can take up to three months to show up and people may be advised to have a repeat test later. Test results are kept strictly confidential and are not reported to the person's GP. Anyone who considers HIV testing should discuss it fully before going ahead and seek support. Other organisations can help, in addition to the clinic's counsellors and doctors – consult the list at the end of this book.

Until recently, life insurance companies asked applicants whether they had been tested for HIV. People feared that anyone who answered yes – even if the test proved negative – would be unlikely to be granted life insurance or even a mortgage. Insurance companies have changed their practices and may now only ask whether applicants are HIV positive.

The criminal justice process

As described in Chapter 2, if a victim chooses to report sexual violence, the police should give them the name of the officer dealing with the investigation and let them know if someone is charged. The police should also keep the victim informed about the progress of the case through the courts and, for example, if the defendant is given bail. The victim should in turn tell the police if they are worried about their attacker intimidating or harassing them, and particularly if incidents occur. It may be possible for victims to have panic alarms installed in their homes or to be given personal alarms to carry with them.

If the police arrest someone for the crime, the victim may be asked to attend an identity parade. If the offender is identified and charged, the police will pass the evidence to the Crown Prosecution Service (CPS) who decide whether to prosecute and, if so, prepare the case for court.

Downgrading of charges and discontinuance of cases

In some cases, the CPS may decide that the evidence is insufficient to bring a charge of rape but may be sufficient to bring a lesser charge, for example of indecent assault. In other cases, the CPS may decide there is insufficient evidence to bring any charge at all and the case is discontinued. The downgrading of charges or discontinuance of cases can make victims feel let down by the criminal justice process in particular and by society in general. Victims can consider bringing a private prosecution (see Chapter 2), but this must be brought within six months of the crime and professional legal advice is essential.

Court and sentencing procedures

Court and sentencing procedures for crimes of sexual violence are broadly similar to those for other crimes (see Chapter 2), but there are some differences. For example, witnesses in cases of sexual violence should automatically be treated by the courts as vulnerable witnesses. The victim's identity must also not be revealed.

In principle, victims of sexual violence should not be asked about their previous sexual history. However, in a small number of specific cases judges may give permission for such questioning. It is understandable that those who do give evidence may be embarrassed about relating intimate details to a room full of strangers, and being cross-examined by the defence counsel can sometimes make them feel as if they are on trial.

A not guilty verdict does not mean that the jury thought the victim was lying – only that there was not enough evidence to convict. If the verdict is guilty, the defending barrister may make a 'plea in mitigation' to try to persuade the judge not to impose the most severe sentence. Sometimes the barrister does this by calling the victim's behaviour into question. This can be particularly distressing in cases of sexual violence. The prosecuting barrister is supposed to challenge such statements and it may help if they already know something about the victim's history. Any information of this kind should be passed to the police who will pass it to the CPS.

Many victims find it helpful to be supported in court during the trial by a volunteer from Victim Support's Witness Service. Despite the ordeal of the court proceedings, not all victims find it a negative experience. Aside from their reactions to the verdict, some feel that publicly standing up and describing how they suffered is empowering and helps the recovery process. Others believe it may prevent other people from suffering similar attacks.

Victims should be kept informed of whether an offender found guilty of rape appeals against their sentence. They should also be contacted by the probation service within two months of sentencing and asked whether they wish to be kept informed about the prisoner's progress and whether they have any anxieties over their eventual release. These should be taken into consideration when the conditions of release are considered.

Media attention

Crimes of sexual violence attract widespread media attention. This is most likely to be focused on crimes committed by strangers and can be helpful in generating information that can help in the police investigation. However, this can give a false impression, as sexual violence is more likely to be committed by someone who knows the victim. This is acknowledged in media coverage of so-called 'date rape', which is not a new phenomenon – it has long been the case that women are raped by men they know.

Some victims may find that talking to the media and acknowledging that they have suffered a crime but are starting to rebuild their life is a valuable part of the recovery process. However, both the victim and the media have to be extremely careful that what is printed or broadcast does not prejudice any future trial. It is therefore best to wait until the trial is over before giving media interviews.

Whatever the story, whenever it is told, it is a serious offence for the media to publish any information or photograph by which victims of sexual violence can be identified.

Simple ways to help

Many people want to help a relative or friend who is a victim of sexual violence but do not know how. Listening without judging is perhaps the most valuable but not the only thing that they can do (see Chapter 1). Pointing the victim in the direction of specialist help as soon as possible is equally important.

Victim Support volunteers can offer emotional support and provide relevant information. They will also be able to discuss such matters as reporting the crime to the police and how to seek medical attention in confidence, and help victims draw upon the experience of other people who have suffered similar crimes.

Volunteers can also give practical assistance by accompanying victims to the police station or to a doctor or to an identity parade or any trial that ensues. If a trial does take place, a volunteer from Victim Support's Witness Service will also be available to help with things like court procedures (see Chapter 2). Another organisation that helps victims of sexual violence is Women's Aid.

Whether or not they take up the offer of specialist help, relatives and friends still have an important role to play in helping the victim to deal with their experience. Although victims may not want to talk about what has happened and people must respect their right to do so and not presume to know how they are feeling, it can be helpful if people say early on that what they want most is for the victim to recover from the experience, but that they are concerned and would like to know whether it is all right to ask how they are every now and then. They may like to tell them that they are there for them whenever they are needed – as long as they mean it.

It is important that relatives and friends do not let their own reactions – which need to be recognised and which they may also require help to cope with – get in the way of helping the direct victim of the crime.

After the shock of any serious crime, even simple tasks can be an added burden. Victims may find it difficult to concentrate, eat, drink or sleep, and someone who offers to do simple shopping, cooking, cleaning, driving people about or even looking after a pet can therefore be a tremendous help. They may also help them to feel safer in their own home by making sure that extra locks and bolts or other security devices are fitted.

Crimes Against People

Overview

- Violent crimes
- How people react to violent crime
  - Immediate reactions
  - Male reactions
  - Trauma and stress
  - Long-term effects
  - Coping with physical injuries
- What happens after violent crime
  - Seeking medical help
  - Contacting the police
  - The criminal justice process
  - Financial consequences
- Domestic violence
  - Deciding what to do
  - Civil procedures
  - Criminal procedures
  - Moving away
  - Financial consequences
  - Victims' reactions
  - Health and safety issues
  - Effects on children
- Racist violence
  - The criminal justice system
  - Recent legislation
  - Civil procedures
  - Landlords' responsibilities
  - Victims' reactions
  - Effects on children
  - Financial consequences
- Homophobic violence
  - Victims' reactions
- Other crimes against people
  - Harassment and threats
  - Deciding what to do
  - Stalking
  - Malicious or obscene communications
  - Victims' reactions
- Simple ways to help

Violent crimes

Violence can include verbal abuse and threats as well as physical assault. It can take place in the home, in the street, at work, at school, or when people are socialising with friends. Violence can also take different forms and be part of a wider pattern of crime, for example domestic or racist violence. Most violent crimes are carried out by someone the victim knows, which only adds to their pain and confusion.

When someone uses, or threatens to use, physical strength or a weapon to impose their will on another person or to take revenge, the victim experiences complex emotional and behavioural responses in addition to any physical injury. As a result, they may find it hard to talk about their feelings. Other people – parents, partners, children, friends – may also be distressed, but feel unable to speak to the victim about their anxiety for fear of adding to their hurt.

In such cases, it can be particularly helpful for victims, and for their family and friends, to talk in confidence to someone from Victim Support. Victim Support has volunteers who are specifically trained to help victims of serious crime and have experience of helping other people from all sections of the community who have suffered similar crimes. Call the Victim Supportline on lo-call number 0845 30 30 900 to talk to a volunteer and/or be put in contact with a local Victim Support scheme. Alternatively, consult the local telephone directory for the number of your local scheme.

How people react to violent crime

Immediate reactions

The victim's immediate reaction to a one-off violent crime will probably be fear and shock, possibly accompanied by trembling or crying (see below for reactions to repeated violence in a domestic, racist or homophobic context). They may be in a state of disbelief at the unreality of the situation and feel out of control. They may feel intense anger towards their attacker, or turn it inward, blaming themselves for getting into the situation from which the attack arose. They may be frustrated or ashamed that they could do nothing to prevent it happening, especially if they were not the only one hurt, and this may affect their self-esteem. They may begin to wonder why they were singled out, or constantly go over the events leading up to the crime, wondering what they might have done to provoke it, and feel guilty, even if they don't know why.

Whatever the circumstances, the victim may have a heightened awareness of possible danger, and fear repetition of the attack. Depending on where it occurred, they may be afraid to go out or to stay in or simply be afraid of the unknown. In some cases, their fears of being attacked again may be realised, especially when their attacker is known to them. According to the *British Crime Survey*, victims of violence are far more likely to be revictimised than victims of other crimes, with one-third of victims experiencing more than one attack in a year. The survey also found that two-thirds of violent crimes are committed by acquaintances or people involved in a domestic relationship.

Victims of violence may therefore become fearful of other people, and adopt a different view of the world and their place in it. They may change their behaviour, for example by trying to ensure that they blend in with rather than stand out from the crowd, or they may withdraw from family or social contact. They may also find that later, unrelated events, for example a television programme or a visit to hospital, trigger disturbing memories of the crime and the feelings it provoked. Different stages of the criminal justice process, such as the onset of a trial, may be another painful reminder of the attack.

Male reactions

While people may be sympathetic towards victims' physical injuries, they may fail to understand the depth of their emotional hurt and anger. Men, who often find it harder than women to talk about their feelings, may find the effects of violence particularly difficult to acknowledge and come to terms with.

This is not helped by other people if they suggest that the man may have contributed in some way to his victimisation, or even be to blame for the crime. It should always be remembered that the only person to blame for a crime is the perpetrator.

Men may find it especially difficult to acknowledge their sense of vulnerability and loss of confidence and/or manage their anger in response to the crime. They may feel guilty about burdening their partners with their anxieties and difficulties. They may feel that their masculinity and self-esteem has been threatened by an attack and wonder whether they defended themselves strongly enough. They may also be anxious about their appearance if they are scarred, and wonder how other people, especially partners, will react to them and what they will assume about their character and behaviour.

Trauma and stress

One problem faced by all victims is how to describe how they really feel following a crime. There is a danger that words like 'trauma' and 'stress' are so much a part of daily language that their specific meaning has been devalued through over-use. But the trauma that victims may experience following crimes of violence and the stress that they feel are very real, and can lead them to believe that there is no way out of their predicament. This may lead to depression, phobia and, in some cases, severe pyschological disturbance.

At its most extreme, victims may suffer from Post Traumatic Stress Disorder (PTSD). A medical condition, diagnosed by a professional doctor or psychiatrist, PTSD is characterised by a cluster of symptoms, some or all of which may be experienced, including violent nightmares, intrusive thoughts of the event or flashbacks, numbing, avoidance, and feelings of arousal, confusion and emptiness. Anyone who feels that a victim may be suffering from PTSD should seek professional medical advice.

Few victims of crime will be diagnosed as having PTSD, but many will share some of the symptoms, for example reliving the event through dreams or daydreams. Knowing what the recognised symptoms of severe stress are, and that they are not unusual, can help them to understand their reactions better and therefore to deal with their experience.

Whatever the nature of the violence, it is important for the victim and their family and friends to put the responsibility for violence where it belongs – with the offender. People have a right to live free from fear, threats and abuse. They are not to blame for what is done to them, and no-one has the right to use violence against them.

Long-term effects

Though the crime may be over in minutes, the victim may spend weeks, months or even years coming to terms with the physical and emotional consequences of it. Some victims may be caught in a cycle of violence and, having been victimised in the past, for example in childhood, may be victimised in the future or use violence themselves. If they choose to use violence, it may be directed against people they know or society in general and the problems may be compounded by the use of alcohol or drugs. Although the number of victims who fall into this category is few, those who do are in need of specialist help.

Helping victims feel safer in their day-to-day life may help to break the cycle. This can include helping them to understand more about managing and avoiding conflict, as well as helping them to improve their personal and home security. Victim Support has volunteers who are specially trained to help victims cope with the effects of serious crime and who can also help them to find out what other sources of help are available.

Coping with physical injuries

Some victims have life-changing physical, as well as emotional, injuries to cope with, following a violent crime. These can range from lacerations and stabbings to loss or impairment of hearing or sight, amnesia, fractures, internal injuries and paralysis. Learning to live with short- and long-term incapacity can be a challenge for the victim and for their family and friends.

Thanks to modern surgical techniques, serious injuries do not necessarily mean someone will be scarred for life, but cuts, fractures, scalds and burns can leave disfiguring marks. Getting used to different physical and especially facial features can be a challenge and looking into the mirror can be distressing for the victim. Disfigurement provides a long-term reminder of the attack and seeing – or imagining – the way other people react can make people acutely self-conscious. Usually the victim – and their family – will experience a whole range of emotions. These range from anger, sadness and despair to thoughts of 'Why me?'. Some people find that they can get over it quite quickly, especially if they are supported by friends and family. Others need more help, for example from the counselling services provided by post-trauma stress clinics or other specialist organisations – consult the list at the end of this book.

What happens after violent crime

Seeking medical attention

The priority following any violent crime is to seek medical attention for any injuries that have been caused. It can help a subsequent court case and/or compensation claim if visible injuries are photographed as evidence. Medical staff treat patients in confidence – even if they suspect an injury has been caused by crime, they should not report it to the police unless the patient requests this.

Contacting the police

If the police have not already been called to the incident, the decision whether or not to report the crime to the police rests with the victim. This can be difficult and it may help to talk it over with a trusted relative or friend first, or with someone from Victim Support. If the attacker is a partner or acquaintance, the decision can be especially difficult.

Reasons given by some people for not reporting assaults include fear of intimidation or retaliation by the offender, fear of not being believed or anxiety about the criminal justice process. Other victims say that reporting helps them to take control over what has happened by not letting the offender 'get away with it', and helps to protect other people from similar attacks.

Victims of robbery are more likely to report crimes to the police, possibly because they are less likely to know their attacker, but also because insurance companies will only meet insurance claims if this is done.

Whether or not they report it to the police, it is a good idea for victims of violent crime to keep a record of what happened, including details such as the time and place of the assault, a description of the attacker or attackers or their name or names if they are known, as well as what was said and done before, during and after the attack, and who witnessed it, together with their contact details.

The criminal justice process

Crimes of violence that are reported to the police have a relatively high chance of being solved and of the offender being prosecuted, not least because the victim may know their attacker.

The victim will probably be the main witness in any court case which follows, and they may find their involvement in the criminal justice process lengthy and stressful, not least because it may not result in a guilty verdict. In the absence of other witnesses willing to come forward, the case may depend on one person's word against another's and the defence may successfully, if unjustly, persuade the jury that the victim was partly to blame for the incident. This may cause victims particular distress, and also fear of intimidation if their attacker is allowed to go free.

For more about the police investigation and criminal justice process and for details of how to claim compensation for injuries received, see Chapter 2.

Financial consequences

It may take months or even years to recover fully from a violent crime or for a case to proceed through the criminal justice system. During this time, the victim may or may not be able to return to work and their financial security, together with that of their family, may suffer as a result. Even victims who return to work may find it difficult to cope or that their work suffers to the point of them having to or, in some cases, being asked to leave.

Victims who are unable to work because of their injuries should tell their employer who may ask them to complete a self-certification form or to get a note from the doctor or hospital describing their health, after which they will usually be entitled to statutory sick pay.

Victims who are not eligible for statutory sick pay who are under retirement age may be able to claim incapacity benefit. Victims who are not eligible for statutory sick pay or incapacity benefit may be able to claim income support. The local benefits agency will provide further details and claim forms.

In addition to possible work-related losses, victims of violence may have to bear direct financial losses connected with the theft by force of cash or property, or damage to property during an assault, which may not be covered by insurance. Victims of violent crime may also have to meet other costs, for example the cost of travelling to medical appointments or court appearances, or, if they feel unsafe at home, of moving house. Additional costs to consider are the cost of increased security and, for example, of using taxis rather than public transport because of fear of further attacks.

Domestic violence

Domestic violence cuts across different crime categories and includes a number of offences that take place in a domestic context. It is generally defined as the physical, sexual, emotional and mental abuse by married or unmarried partners or ex-partners, and includes assault, sexual violence, threats to kill, murder and attempted murder, as well as burglary and criminal damage.

Mostly committed by men against women, violence can occur in other domestic relationships in which men are abused by women, children are abused by parents, parents are abused by children, and gay and lesbian men and women are abused by same-sex partners. The key issue is the misuse of power and exercise of control by one person over the other.

The control may be enforced by behaviours which are not always criminal in themselves, but are aimed at restricting someone's privacy and liberty. These may include: manipulation; verbal abuse; curtailment of freedom; restricting contact with family and friends; opening personal mail; screening telephone calls; witholding and controlling money; and using other people – children and adults – to enforce the victim's compliance.

It is estimated that one woman in four suffers domestic violence at some time in their lives and that domestic violence accounts for one-quarter of all violent crime. In addition, it is estimated that two women are killed by their current or former partners every week.

Domestic violence incidents can escalate in frequency and severity over time, with victims enduring many attacks and waiting years before seeking help. It occurs in all sections of society, irrespective of social class, family income, level of education, occupation or ethnic background. Other people suffer too – it is thought that more than 50 per cent of children in households that suffer domestic violence witness abuse of their mother and/or personally experience violence.

Deciding what to do

Some people may find it hard to understand why victims of domestic violence do not simply leave their abuser, but this is often far easier to say than to do. Keeping the victim dependent on them and depriving them of outside support, as well as an independent livelihood, is part of the abuser's control. In addition to financial difficulties and having nowhere else to live, victims may fear that their children will suffer more if they left home, or even fear that they would be taken from them. It is also true that many victims still love their abuser but simply want the abuse to stop.

Deciding to take action against domestic violence marks the moment at which the victim starts to regain control over their life. However, this is a difficult decision and victims should discuss the issues first with a trusted relative or friend, a doctor or a specialist organisation. Accessing outside help can be difficult, not only because of the need for secrecy, but also because of the number of different agencies that may be involved.

Volunteers from organisations like Victim Support and Women's Aid are specially trained to help victims in these circumstances and may arrange to meet the victim away from home, at a safe time and place, so that they can discuss their options in confidence. These may include choosing between: trying to persuade the perpetrator to change their ways; trying to have them removed from the house;

leaving home themselves and taking children with them; or putting up with even worse violence.

Many victims find it hard to access the information that they need to plan their escape, but this is particularly true for victims from ethnic minority groups for whom English may be a second language. For these women, attitudes to marriage in their own communities may make it even harder to assert their right to life without violence and fear, for example, if separation is regarded as shameful, whatever the circumstances.

Civil procedures

Victims can seek legal protection from domestic violence through the civil law (see Chapter 2). This involves contacting a solicitor to apply for a court order or 'injunction', which orders or forbids the perpetrator to act or to not act in a certain way for a period of time.

To help them seek legal advice victims may be entitled to receive financial help from the Community Legal Service Fund and/or free legal advice under the 'green form scheme' (see Chapter 2). The Community Legal Service Fund is currently in the process of taking over from the Legal Aid Board. Emergency funding may be available for people in immediate danger.

Criminal procedures

Victims can also seek legal protection from domestic violence through the criminal law by reporting the violence to the police. Domestic violence is now much better understood by the police and by other criminal justice organisations. Most police forces have domestic violence officers, usually women, who specialise in this kind of work. With the victim's permission, they may also refer them to Victim Support.

If a complaint is reported to the police the perpetrator will be interviewed and possibly charged. They may then appear in court and either be remanded in custody or released on bail, pending a trial in which the victim will be a witness. However, the perpetrator may also be released without charge, or after being cautioned. In some cases, being charged is sufficient to make the offender want to change their behaviour, for example, through attending a violence control programme. In other cases, it may put victims in danger of retaliation.

In such instances, or if the case is sent for trial and the perpetrator is meanwhile granted bail, victims may find it necessary to protect themselves and their family by leaving home or increasing their personal security. Even if bail is granted on condition that the offender lives apart from or does not contact the victim, they may still be in danger if the offender breaks those conditions. Many areas have schemes whereby vulnerable victims can have alarms fitted in their homes, for example panic alarms or alarms that activate a recording, which can be used as evidence in later court proceedings. They may also be loaned items such as personal alarms or mobile 999 phones. The police or an organisation like Victim Support can provide details of what help is available.

Moving away
The police can put domestic violence victims in touch with agencies who can help find a safe place for them and their children to go. In these circumstances, any local authority that the victim applies to has a duty to find them temporary accommodation – they are not classed as 'intentionally homeless'.

Refuges, whose addresses are kept secret to protect residents, are another source of accommodation. There are nearly 450 refuges in England and Wales. Conditions vary – there is often not much privacy, some are full to the limit, and the nearest may be miles away. But refuges offer victims an invaluable breathing space so that they can decide on a plan of action and, with help, rebuild their lives.

A victim who is planning to leave home in these circumstances should take with them essential documents, such as birth and marriage certificates, benefit and rent books, passports, savings books, cheque book and cards, and their driving licence.

Financial consequences
The financial consequences of violence are even more significant in domestic cases, where financial dependence is one of the perpetrator's weapons of control. For victims who do not work

outside the home, beginning training and/or getting a job can be
one way that victims start to rebuild their self-esteem and their lives.
However, some perpetrators become even more violent if they
think that, as a result of this, they are losing power over the victim.

While some victims who work outside the home feel that work
provides a source of support as well as financial independence,
others find that the stress caused by domestic violence prevents
them from doing their job well or even at all. Victims who are forced
to give up work may therefore suffer from loss of support as well as
financially.

Short-term crisis or budgeting loans may be available to help
victims who are already receiving benefit to escape from domestic
violence. Community care grants may be available to help victims
in other circumstances. Contact the local benefits' office for more
details.

Victims' reactions

Apart from the effect of physical injuries, most victims find that
living in fear is one of the most serious emotional consequences of
domestic violence. They may experience guilt and wonder whether
in some way they may be responsible, or shame if they know other
people are aware of what has happened. Other victims may be
further humiliated if, under the threat of violence, they have given
in to domestic or sexual demands that they know they should not
have to tolerate. As a result, they may feel demoralised, trapped,
isolated from their family, friends and community, and unable to do
anything about it – precisely how the perpetrator wants them to
feel.

Health and safety issues

In addition to physical injuries, such as bruises, lacerations, broken
bones and woundings, the stress of living in the shadow of violence
may seriously affect victims' health. They may become anxious or
depressed and, in the long term, this can lead to serious physical and
mental health problems, or even alcohol or drug abuse. One way to
begin to end the abuse is for victims to talk about the full nature of
the problem if they do have to go to their doctor or a hospital

accident and emergency department for treatment. Medical staff will talk to them in confidence and can put them in contact with other people who can help.

The stress – and the danger – associated with domestic violence can be all the greater when victims are at the point of breaking free. If the perpetrator, for example, becomes aware that the victim is seeking help, then they may try to discourage them by threats or acts of further violence towards them, their children or their supporters. The fear and guilt that this can arouse can be especially difficult for the victim to bear.

The immediate victim of domestic violence is not the only person at risk of violence from their abuser – their children, relatives and friends may also suffer; fear of this only adds to the victim's distress.

Effects on children

Even if children are not attacked themselves, they are likely to have witnessed violence and to be seriously affected by it. As a result they may become depressed and withdrawn or anxious and hyperactive, have difficulty sleeping or concentrating, or develop stress-related illnesses. They may also demonstrate regressive behaviours, such as bed-wetting, become 'clingy' or aggressive, and have difficulties at school and/or with other children, some of which may develop into long-term behaviour problems.

Children may sadly also grow up to imitate the aggressive behaviour they have witnessed and learned in childhood. It is therefore especially important to explain to children what is going on and to seek help to protect them.

Racist violence

Like domestic violence, racist violence cuts across different crime categories and is an umbrella term for a number of offences against members of ethnic minority groups. The offences range from criminal damage to property and possessions to verbal and physical abuse, threats, physical and sexual assault, arson and murder. Racist violence may be preceded by verbal and non-verbal behaviour that is not always criminal, but may amount to racist harassment over a period of time, for example hostile looks, name calling and insults, graffiti, leaving rubbish outside a door or by a desk, putting excrement through the letter box, malicious complaints, letter writing and phone calls. It can happen to anyone, from young children to elderly people, whether they are alone or with friends and family, and whether they are at work or at home.

Racist violence can affect people from all backgrounds, in all areas. Motivated by the perpetrator's prejudice against an individual on account of their colour, race, creed, nationality or ethnic origin, racist violence in the UK is most often committed by white people against black and ethnic minority peoples. The perpetrators include men and women of all ages, from children to pensioners, who may act alone or with friends and family members. Even if members of the perpetrators' own communities do not engage in such crimes themselves, the fact that they do not openly oppose them may be taken by perpetrators as validation of their criminal behaviour. Whoever is responsible, wherever it takes place, racist violence is a double injustice because its victims are victims of hatred as well as of crime.

The criminal justice system

Like domestic violence, incidents of racist violence can be of a serious and prolonged nature, escalating in frequency and severity over time. Victims may endure many attacks and wait years before seeking help. According to some estimates, only 1 crime in 20 is reported to the police.

Many victims from ethnic minority groups choose not to report crimes because they know their attackers and have to continue living and studying or working alongside them and are afraid of retaliation, particularly if the case goes to court. Some victims are also suspicious of the police or fear that they will be blamed or not believed or that there is not much the police can effectively do to help. Others may be worried that they may even be detained and treated as if they were offenders rather than victims. Language may be an extra barrier preventing victims from reporting incidents to the police.

Victims may be victimised a second time if they feel that the criminal justice system is not open to them, fails to take their allegations seriously or fails to prosecute the offender. Although most service providers are working to address the problem, in some parts of the system – and of society in general – discrimination is institutional. In such cases, discrimination results from long-established systems, practices and procedures that have the effect, if not always the intention, of depriving ethnic minority groups of equality of opportunity and access to society's resources.

Not all crimes against victims from ethnic minority groups are racially motivated and some criminals target people precisely because they are less likely to report crimes to the police. A crime may also not appear to an outsider to be racially motivated, whereas the victim may be convinced that it is so, because of the history of harassment they have faced.

Whatever the motivation, people from ethnic minority groups are disproportionately at risk of crime. According to the *British Crime Survey*, people of Asian ethnic origin are two-thirds more likely to be burgled than white people, and people of black ethnic origin are a third more likely. Other research shows that, while two per cent of the population is of black ethnic origin and three per cent is of Asian, black people comprised eight per cent of homicide victims in 1998/99, and Asian people comprised six per cent.

Recent legislation

The Crime and Disorder Act 1998 introduced new crimes of assault, criminal damage, public order and harassment that carry higher maximum penalties where it can be shown that the offence was racially aggravated. These place a duty on the police, and on local authorities, to give greater emphasis to racist crimes, which it is hoped will encourage more victims to report crimes. Local authorities and the police are also required to draw up and implement a strategy to reduce all crime and disorder in their area, including racist crime.

The Macpherson report of *The Stephen Lawrence Inquiry*, published in 1999, broke new ground in highlighting the way crimes of racist violence are dealt with by the criminal justice system. In particular it defines institutionalised racism and recommends that every organisation and institution should examine their policies and practices to guard against disadvantaging any section of the community. It also recommends that measures should be introduced to encourage the reporting of racist incidents to the police and the recording of those that are reported as racist.

Many police forces have independently appointed ethnic minority liaison officers to help them deal with racist crimes. Other agencies working within the criminal justice system are also required to collect information about how members of ethnic minorities are treated by the criminal justice process. Vulnerable witnesses can now also be helped to give evidence in court (see Chapter 2).

Civil procedures

One of the problems in prosecuting racist crimes is the difficulty in proving that a crime was motivated by racism. In the criminal courts the standard of proof is that the case must be proved 'beyond reasonable doubt', whereas in the civil courts cases must be proved 'on the balance of probabilities'. Victims who feel that they cannot seek redress for crimes they have suffered through the criminal law may take action themselves through the civil courts to claim damages for injuries received (see Chapter 2). This is not an easy decision to make and professional legal advice should be sought.

Landlords' responsibilities

In addition to taking legal action to support tenants who are victims of racist crime, landlords are responsible for repairing any damage to property that may have been caused. They may also help by providing extra security measures, such as panic alarms or additional locks and bolts. Victims who are home-owners will have to claim for the cost of repairing damage through their household insurance. But any victim who is vulnerable and on limited means may be able to have additional security measures fitted as part of a local crime prevention project. Victim Support and Neighbourhood Watch Schemes or the police crime prevention officer can help.

Victims' reactions

Racist crimes have a serious and long-term impact on victims and the cumulative effect of repeated lower level incidents can be just as traumatic as isolated more serious crimes. Victims of racist crime experience the same reactions as victims of all crimes (see Chapter 1), most commonly, anger, shock and fear. Fear is especially important because it constrains and makes a misery of victims' daily lives, affecting the way they think, feel and act. It also affects where victims live, work and study, the route they take to work or school, the time of day they go out, where they shop, and what sport and leisure activities they participate in. Fear may be long-lasting and devastating, affecting both the direct victims of such crimes and other members of their community.

In extreme cases, victims of racist crime may be afraid to go out alone, especially at night. This withdrawal from social contact is all the more serious for victims who may already feel isolated, either because of the community in which they live, or because their first language is not English. Other victims whose homes have been attacked may be afraid to stay in because the one place they felt safe has been violated.

The emotional impact of racist violence, in addition to the pain caused by any physical injuries received, cannot be over-estimated. Such crimes are not just an attack on an individual, but also an attack on the victim's background, culture and heritage, and the effects are made worse by the knowledge that someone was attacked simply because of who they are. In response, victims feel angry but powerless, which brings its own sense of injustice and makes it particularly hard for them to protect themselves.

As a result, victims may find it hard to sleep, they may have nightmares, they may be unusually startled, afraid or easily distracted. Victims may feel demoralised, depressed and in despair, and the stress associated with this can put added strain on existing medical conditions. It can particularly affect the way victims think about themselves, for example diminishing their self-esteem. Some victims are so traumatised that they are unable to live a normal life.

Effects on children

Children need particular help in coping with the effects of racist crimes. They may be picked on or bullied at or near school, either personally or as a member of a victimised household or community. They may find it particularly difficult to understand why they are so disliked and this may seriously affect their developing sense of personal identity.

As in cases of domestic violence, children who are direct or indirect victims of racist crime may become depressed and withdrawn, or anxious and hyperactive. They may have difficulty sleeping or concentrating, or develop stress-related illnesses. They may also demonstrate regressive behaviours, such as bed-wetting, or become 'clingy' or aggressive, and have difficulties at school and/or with other children, some of which may develop into long-term behaviour problems.

Parents should be encouraged to talk to teachers, so that they will understand if children are behaving differently, and can take action if there are signs of racist behaviour in school. Most victims find that accessing outside support is a vital step in taking back control of their lives and feeling safer in the local and the wider community.

In cases where victims want to report racist violence to the police but do not speak English as a first language, children who speak English fluently may be asked to interpret on their behalf. This can place an inappropriate responsibility on a child, who may be asked to describe distressing events and feelings, at the same time as they are trying to cope with the effects of the crime on themselves.

Financial consequences

Victims of racist crime may have to cope with significant financial expenditure, in addition to the emotional and physical cost of the crime(s). At its most extreme, victims may be made homeless or forced to leave an area or feel so unsafe that they choose to move away. Whether they are tenants or home-owners, the cost is substantial.

Other costs that they may have to bear include the cost of repairing damage, cleaning or painting over graffiti, replacing possessions and increasing home and personal security. Victims may or may not have insurance to cover these – even if they do, there may be costs associated with a loss in no-claims bonuses or a policy excess. Victims may also have to pay for the cost of travelling to medical appointments or court, or simply of protecting themselves from further attacks by taking taxis rather than public transport.

Homophobic violence

Like domestic and racist violence, homophobic violence cuts across different crime categories and includes a number of offences against gay men and lesbians by people prejudiced against them. Crimes can range from criminal damage, verbal and physical abuse, intimidation and harassment to sexual violence, physical assault, arson and murder.

Lesbians and gay men may also be victims of crimes with no homophobic motivation. As with racist crime, some offenders may take advantage of the fact that gay and lesbian victims of both homophobic and non-homophobic crime are less likely to report crimes to the police. Apart from fear of retaliation by their attackers, some are suspicious of the police in general, or fear that they will be blamed or not believed. Others are worried that reporting the offence and any court case that ensues may force them to reveal details of their lifestyle that they prefer to keep private – victims' anonymity is only protected in cases relating to sexual offences. Lesbians who are victims of domestic violence may have the additional fear that their children may be taken away from them if their sexual orientation becomes known.

Police in many areas are working to build links with gay and lesbian communities, and are beginning to introduce special procedures for dealing with homophobic crimes. Organisations that can help victims cope with such crimes include Victim Support and Lesbian and Gay Switchboard – see the contacts section at the end of this book.

Victims' reactions
Crimes motivated by homophobia are not just attacks on an individual – they are also an attack on someone's lifestyle and culture. As with racist crime, they can leave the victim feeling

frightened, demoralised, depressed and in despair. They can particularly diminish the victim's self-esteem and make them feel isolated, powerless and angry. Other members of the gay or lesbian community may also be affected and live in fear of further attacks.

It is particularly hard for victims to defend themselves against such incidents and the effects of the crime are made worse by the knowledge that someone was attacked simply because of who they are. Not only does this appear unjust, victims may feel they are denied access to criminal justice because they fear that reporting the crime might lead them to risk retaliation.

Other crimes against people

Harassment and threats

Harassment is when one or more people cause a persistent nuisance to another, for example one that makes them afraid or forces them to move house. This may be directed towards a member of a group of people, for example an ethnic minority group or gay men and lesbians, or towards one or more members of a family, for example as a result of a neighbour dispute, or towards an individual, for example in the case of sexual harassment or stalking.

Whatever its motivation, harassment can be in the form of a series of persistent minor incidents, as well as individual or multiple serious attacks. Although the actions involved may or may not be criminal, it is always an offence to intentionally cause a person harassment, alarm or distress by using threatening, abusive or insulting words or behaviour. It is also an offence to intentionally cause a person harassment, alarm or distress by displaying any writing or sign that is threatening, abusive or insulting, or to intimidate someone, or threaten them with harm.

Harassment may sometimes amount to another offence. For example, sexual harassment, whereby one person constantly makes advances of a sexual nature to another who has made it clear that advances are unwelcome, can amount to indecent assault. Similarly, harassing someone by persistently following, telephoning or stalking them can amount to inflicting grievous bodily harm.

Though it can be difficult to prove and bring charges, a threat to commit any violent act is itself a crime, provided that the person who makes the threat has the ability and intention to carry it out.

Deciding what to do

Victims of harassment should make sure that someone else knows what is happening. This may be a trusted relative, friend, workplace official, community representative or the police. Although victims may be reluctant to report incidents because they fear they are not serious enough, the police have now been given more powers to tackle harassment through the civil and criminal law.

The Protection from Harassment Act 1997 introduced new criminal offences to punish conduct causing harassment, alarm or distress, and fear of violence. The Crime and Disorder Act 1998 introduced the Anti-Social Behaviour Order (ASBO), a civil court order, backed by criminal sanctions if it is breached, which prohibits behaviour that causes harassment, alarm or distress. Applications for an ASBO have to be supported with evidence, but this is gathered and presented by the police or local council – not the victim.

Victims of harassment who know the perpetrator's name may also apply for a civil order or 'injunction' themselves (see Chapter 2). This orders or forbids the perpetrator to do or not do certain things for a period of time. Applicants may be entitled to financial help through the Community Legal Service Fund (formerly Legal Aid), but applications take time to be decided and are not always successful. The victim may therefore have to finance the action at their own expense.

Victims of harassment can also ask the local council for help. For example, if the harassment involves noise nuisance, the local council may be able to prosecute the offender under environmental health regulations. And if the victim and the perpetrator are tenants of the local authority or a housing association, the perpetrator may be in breach of their tenancy agreement and be liable to eviction. This is not always easy, however, because relations between the parties may become even worse while the matter is investigated. It may also be that the victim does not know who is harassing them.

Both the local council and the police need evidence before they can act. Victims should therefore record all incidents, noting who is harassing them, when and where incidents take place, what happened, who witnessed them, and who they were reported to. In some cases, it may be worth considering mediation (see Chapter 2).

Stalking

Stalking is generally regarded as harassment and may be dealt with as above. According to the actions involved, it may also be dealt with by the criminal law as assault, if it can be proved that psychological harm has been caused, or as an offence under laws regarding the sending of malicious communications or telephone calls.

Stalking can affect anyone, men or women, from celebrities to members of the general public, who may or may not know the perpetrator. Some stalkers are taking revenge for a broken relationship, other stalkers believe that the object of their obsession has or would like to have a relationship with them.

One of the difficulties with prosecuting stalkers under the criminal law has been proving they intended to cause harm – many perpetrators say they have no desire to hurt their victim and they may even believe their attentions are welcomed. It can also be hard to prove why, for example, the daily sending of flowers or gifts is a malicious action. Such 'gifts' are in reality a symbol and constant reminder of the perpetrator's control.

The Protection from Harassment Act 1997 has sought to address this problem and is a unique piece of criminal legislation in that the prosecution does not have to prove the defendant's intention for them to be found guilty of the crime.

Malicious or obscene communications

Making malicious telephone calls or other forms of communication is in itself a criminal offence, but in some cases it may also be treated as harassment or assault, if the victim is left to fear that force may be used against them.

British Telecom advises people who receive unwanted calls, however upsetting they are, to try to remain calm and silent – the caller may feel encouraged by an emotional response or the victim entering into a conversation. If the calls are silent, or from a 'heavy breather', the victim should place the handset down beside the telephone and ignore it for a few minutes before gently replacing it.

Service providers are becoming more and more aware of the extreme distress that malicious calls can cause. They will usually change a telephone number quickly and free of charge. In addition, modern telephone equipment and services allow telephone users to screen their calls more easily, and in cases of persistent telephone nuisance, specially trained investigators will work with the victim to trace the calls and if necessary bring in the police. For details call 0800 661441.

Victims' reactions

Whatever their motivation, harassment, stalking and malicious calls can have a devastating effect on people's lives and a series of minor incidents may have as great an impact on a victim as a single more serious attack. The effects are similar to those noted for violent crime, for example fear, anger and distress. Victims may become anxious about being victimised in other ways. This is particularly true of female victims of obscene telephone calls who may worry that the perpetrator may one day attack them. Although there is no evidence to suggest that they are at greater risk, the fact that the victim knows they are part of the perpetrator's fantasy can be extremely disturbing and intimidating.

Victims can be particularly upset by the repeated nature of such incidents and suffer from the prolonged nature of the perpetrator's control over their lives. Many victims of stalking, for example, may be stalked for years, in public places, at work, at home, and more recently on the internet, to the extent that the victim feels helpless and unable to live a normal life. What is especially distressing is that the perpetrator either knows or finds out so much about the victim, yet the victim may know little about them. In some cases, the perpetrator's actions may extend to the victim's family, children and friends, and victims may live in fear that they and their loved ones are at risk of harm.

Simple ways to help

Many people want to help a relative or friend who is a victim of violence, harassment, stalking or threats. Listening without judging and in confidence is perhaps the most valuable thing they can do. This is especially so in domestic violence cases where it is vitally important for their own and the victim's safety not to let the offender – or any third party – know the victim is seeking help.

Reassurance is equally important to victims who may feel that people fail to believe them or take their physical and emotional injuries seriously. Victims need to know that the crime they have suffered was not their fault and that they are not alone in being victimised.

Concern for the victim's current safety may also lead friends and relatives to discuss how the victim can maximise their personal and household security. Practical tasks, such as fitting additional locks and bolts, may help, as can accompanying them if they decide to report the crime to the police, or to return to the place where they were attacked.

Helping victims to find information about, and access to, other sources of help is also useful and can help the victim to understand their options. But victims should never be pressured into making decisions, especially about whether to leave a violent relationship. In such cases, only the victim can decide whether to seek outside help or what to do.

Victim Support can put victims of violence, harassment or stalking in touch with volunteers who are specially trained in serious crime and in domestic violence. Other organisations that can help include Women's Aid, the Commission for Racial Equality, and Lesbian and Gay Helpline.

6

Crimes Against Property

Overview

Property crimes

There is no such thing as 'just' property crime – whether the crime is burglary, criminal damage, fraud, theft or arson, anyone can be deeply affected by what can feel like the violation of their personal space and/or belongings. Research has shown that in nearly nine out of ten burglaries in which burglars gain entry to a property the victims are emotionally affected by the crime and in more than one-third of cases they are 'very much' affected.

It is a myth that wealthy people are most at risk. Studies show that the people most vulnerable to property crimes are those living in economically disadvantaged households in which the head of the household is unemployed, household income is low, the home is rented and there is no car.

But fear of crime blights many people's lives, regardless of their financial means. Although few people come face to face with burglars in their home – violent or threatening confrontations occur in about only one-tenth of burglaries – someone is at home in nearly half of all incidents. Children whose homes have been burgled may be particularly frightened of the burglar returning and may develop short-term or even long-term emotional problems as a result.

Property offences, including thefts of and from cars, are the most common crimes committed in England and Wales. Car crimes are not referred to Victim Support by the police, but victims who are concerned by any crime can contact Victim Support directly by telephoning the lo-call Victim Supportline number, 0845 30 30 900. The victims of other property crimes will be sent a Victim Support leaflet describing how people may react and giving information about the practical things that should be done following such crimes. They will also be contacted with the offer of support from a trained Victim Support volunteer to help them deal with the experience. This may be by allowing them the opportunity to talk about such feelings as fear, shock, distress and anger, and providing reassurance that these are normal and even healthy reactions. It might also be by offering practical help and information about how property can be repaired or replaced, as well as ways in which future crimes may be prevented.

Victims of crime may contact Victim Support themselves at any time – either immediately after a crime happens, or months or years later, for example if reminders of the offence cause them distress. However, victims often find the most useful time to accept the offer of help is within a day or two of the crime.

How people react to property crime

Arson

When criminal damage is caused by fire the offence is arson and the maximum penalty for anyone found guilty of the crime is imprisonment for life. The sentence acknowledges the exceptional danger involved – victims may lose all their property, be made homeless, injured, or suffer a very painful death.

It follows that the effects of the arson, in addition to the general effects of crime described in Chapter 1 and the particular effects of homicide in Chapter 3, can be catastrophic. What can make it even harder for the survivors to bear is the uncertainty of not knowing, until the police and fire service's investigation is complete, whether or not the fire was caused deliberately. This can mean weeks, sometimes months, of additional anguish, during which victims may live in fear of further attacks. Arson can also be motivated by racism and be the culmination of a series of incidents of racist harassment. In addition to having to cope with the devastating effects of the immediate crime, survivors may live in constant fear of further attacks.

As with many crimes, the police questioning has to take account of the possibility that the fire was started deliberately, even by someone who lived in the home. This cannot be avoided, but it does not help the survivors' recovery if they feel that they, or someone in their family, are under suspicion.

Burglary

Although for some people burglary amounts to no more than the inconvenience of an insurance claim, it is usually about far more than loss of property. What is significant about the crime and its impact on victims is that it involves intrusion into the home. This is particularly the case if the burglar has opened drawers and wardrobes and left everything in a mess. In general, the more untidy the burglary or the more evident the signs of intrusion, the more painful the effects may be. Some burglars will vandalise the home in addition to stealing from it. Although this is rare, it can be very distressing if it happens.

Whatever the degree of disturbance, the intrusion makes the victim feel that their personal space – the one place they felt safe – has been violated. This is in addition to their feelings of loss for both physical possessions, particularly irreplaceable ones of sentimental value, and for less tangible things, such as peace of mind and personal security. To some people, the feelings of loss amount to a grief reaction similar to bereavement.

The real value of property lost or damaged during a burglary is relative to the financial means of the victim and their ability to replace or repair it. The child who loses a pair of trainers they saved for months to buy may be more deeply affected than an adult whose watch is stolen, which they may feel is regrettable but replaceable.

Victims who were at home at the time of the burglary may face the additional stress of imagining what might have happened if they had confronted the burglar. Whatever the circumstances, any victim may suffer emotionally after the crime and in some cases this may lead to severe psychological disturbance.

Among the victim's emotional reactions to burglary may be anger, shock, disorientation, disbelief and fear. Although the only person responsible for the crime is the offender, the victim may still feel that they were in some way to blame. Their emotional upset may be shown in their restlessness, sleeplessness or irritability, and they may be depressed and have intrusive recollections of what has been stolen and its significance. All of these reactions may be made worse by sudden reminders of the event, such as reading or hearing about similar crimes, or, where applicable, having to deal with another stage of an insurance claim or the criminal justice process.

Men and women may react differently in their attempts to restore order and regain control over their lives. Women may respond by frantic cleaning of the house and men by excessive checking of household security. Men and women also appear to differ in their emotional response to burglary: while women will focus on fear, men will often show anger. There is some evidence to suggest that women experience more distress in relation to burglary than men, possibly because they traditionally have a stronger emotional and/or domestic bond with the home. In such cases, their partners may fail to understand and support them at the time they are most in need.

Victims who live alone may be particularly fearful of being burgled again and may stay at home and withdraw from family and social contacts. But this is not always the case, and it is wrong to assume that an elderly woman who has always lived alone will suffer more than a young man who is living alone for the first time. What matters is the support structure and life experience that the individual can draw upon. Young men who are conditioned into believing the stereotype of the 'macho' male may find it particularly difficult to admit their feelings.

Many victims of burglary are unprepared for the time it may take to sort out insurance claims and make good any damage caused. If property is left insecure during this period, it heightens the victim's sense of fear at the time they may be feeling most vulnerable. Whether or not their home is secured, victims of burglary may be afraid to leave it unattended and, if they do, be wary of what they will find when they return. Such fears can last for months or even years. They may also be suspicious of those who live near them, wondering if they were responsible for the crime, or if they saw what happened and did nothing to prevent it. As a result they may feel that their trust in human nature is severely challenged by their experience.

The effects on children
No-one should under-estimate the serious impact that burglary can have on children (see Chapter 7). Children can be particularly upset at the thought of an intruder in their home – especially in their room – and may feel particularly insecure and concerned that they will return. Many victims are disturbed by the fact that, while they know very little about the burglar, the burglar may have learned much about them. Given their powers of imagination, children can be especially disturbed by wondering who invaded their home and why. Yet the fact is that offenders are usually far less threatening than victims perceive, and they usually pick their victims at random and not by design.

Children's anxiety may manifest itself in changes of behaviour, for example 'clinginess', bed-wetting, a refusal to sleep alone or an obsession with checking the home's security. Children within the same family, like adults, may also react differently from one another. Most children recover in a relatively short time, but parents may find it useful to discuss how to help their children with someone from Victim Support, a teacher, doctor or other professional.

Students are particularly at risk of burglary, not least because they may live in low-rent, multiple-occupancy accommodation often targeted by criminals. It is likely that they also possess the kind of hi-fi and computer equipment that the opportunist thief is looking for. Away from home and alone for the first time, students may be more naïve about personal security and find it even harder to cope with the experience of being burgled.

People who know never say that burglary is a trivial offence that has little impact on its victims. But because some people fail to take its effects seriously, those victims who remain disturbed after the initial shock of the crime has subsided may think that they are unusual and may fail to talk about their feelings and fears, or be embarrassed about asking for help in coping with them. It is important that they know they are not unusual, and that there are people who can – and want – to help, including Victim Support.

Burglary by artifice

Victims of doorstep fraudsters may feel foolish and especially suffer from self-blame following a burglary. But self-blame is a common reaction after many kinds of crime and the blame properly belongs to the offender not the victim. It may help if the victim can come to understand that it was very natural to be taken in on the first occasion, but that they can take action to guard against it happening again.

Victims of this kind of burglary, who are often more vulnerable members of society, for example elderly or disabled people, may particularly feel that their trust in society as a whole has been threatened by the crime. They may also feel vulnerable to further incidents.

Theft

How people may react to theft is similar to the reactions to burglary described above. Anger and fear are common reactions, but theft is also about loss, and although the financial hardship that theft can cause should never be under-estimated, the value of the stolen property may bear little relation to the significance of the loss for the victim. A stolen handbag or wallet can, for example, contain irreplaceable photographs or mementos, stolen jewellery can deprive the victim of cherished memories, and stolen papers can represent someone's life's work.

While the thief's primary motivation is usually money, a stolen handbag or wallet may also contain a driving licence or other document that gives the victim's identity and address. The victim may therefore feel vulnerable and fear that they are at risk of further crimes, such as burglary, stalking or even assault, because the offender knows where they live and may even have their keys. In such cases, it should be a priority to have locks changed.

Victims of theft may also fear being criticised for their apparent carelessness in leaving their personal property unattended. This may be accompanied by self-blame and a lowering of self-esteem. They may also be distressed because the victim feels that someone noticed their vulnerability and waited for an opportunity to strike. If the theft took place in a work context, the victim may fear the reactions of employers and colleagues and think that the theft will reflect on their competence. Again, it is important to remember that the only person responsible for the crime is the offender.

Criminal damage

What can hurt victims most about criminal damage to private property is the waste that it implies. Whether motivated by jealousy, hatred, lack of respect or lack of empathy for the victim, it represents the offender's deliberate intention to destroy or damage something that they value and have probably worked hard to achieve.

Victims will often take the damage personally and interpret it as a particular sign of hatred towards them. Not knowing who is responsible may cause them particular anxiety. But, although in some cases the damage may be targeted as part of a wider pattern of harassment or bullying, offenders may also attack at random.

The pain that can be caused by damage that is intended personally, for example offensive graffiti that deliberately points at the victim, may be extreme. Aside from shame and embarrassment, the victim may withdraw from social contact with their local community, either because they fear other people may share the views expressed, or because they fear other people will be talking about them. All victims may live in fear of further incidents and some may feel forced to move house as a consequence. In such cases, a volunteer from Victim Support will be able to provide emotional support to help the victim(s) deal with the experience, as well as practical information to help them cope, for example about about how to get the graffiti removed.

What happens after property crime

Contacting the police

Victims of property crimes are more likely than victims of other crimes to report incidents to the police. This may be because a crime like arson is so serious and life-threatening that victims want the police to do everything in their power to catch the offender. Alternatively, it may be because insurance companies require a crime such as burglary, theft or criminal damage to be reported before they will process a claim for stolen or damaged goods.

Common reasons that some victims give for not reporting property crimes to the police include that the incident was too trivial, or that it was unlikely that the offender would be caught. Other people may decide not to report because they fear that doing so might expose details of their lifestyle, which they choose to keep private, to the police. Alternatively, the crime might be part of a wider pattern of harassment, for example on account of their ethnic background or sexual orientation, and victims may fear that problems will escalate if they involve the police.

If a property crime is reported, a police officer will be sent to investigate (see Chapter 2). If arson is suspected, a full-scale investigation will be mounted. For other property crimes, depending on the evidence available, the police officer may still call for expert assistance from the CID or a scenes of crime officer who may, for example, take fingerprints or other forensic evidence. For this reason it is important to leave things exactly as they are – however distressing this may be – until the police have completed their task. Fingerprints may also have to be taken from residents, in order to eliminate them from the forensic enquiry results.

If they have not already been told by the investigating officer, the victim should be contacted to indicate whether the police will investigate the crime further, or whether it will be left on file, pending further information. If the offender is caught and prosecution goes ahead, the victim may be asked to appear as a witness in the trial, which, depending on the nature of the offence, will take place in either the magistrates' court or Crown Court (see Chapter 2). Witnesses in Crown Court trials may find it useful to accept the offer of support from Victim Support's Witness Service. This service is currently being expanded to operate in the magistrates' courts too.

However, with the exception of burglaries in which the offender carries a weapon, retail theft, handling stolen goods, and forgery, the police are far less likely to clear up property crimes than violent crimes against people. As a result, fewer victims of property crimes become involved in the criminal justice process.

Those who do may find it useful to take part in supervised victim-offender meetings, if they are later offered the opportunity by the police or probation service (see Chapter 2). Many offenders fail to think of their victims and, in the case of property crimes, often assume that they are covered by insurance and will not be bothered by the crime. Victim-offender meetings allow victims to tell their offenders exactly how the crime affected them and allow offenders the opportunity to learn from the experience, in the hope that they will be less likely to reoffend. They also allow victims to receive answers to their questions, for example why they were 'singled out' by the offender. Many victims who take part in such meetings say that they are a valuable exercise because they allow them to see that their offender is less threatening and much weaker than they had perceived.

Alternative accommodation

If the victim has been made homeless by property crime, one of the first priorities is to find alternative accommodation. The police will usually put people in touch with the local council who have a duty to find temporary accommodation for them. However, as public housing stock is limited, transfers to permanent alternative accommodation can take months or even years.

Insurance cover

Provided the victim has cover in place, the insurance company should be contacted as soon as possible following a property crime. A list of items that have been stolen or damaged needs to be prepared for both the police and the insurance company, and both should be informed if other items are later discovered missing or damaged. Losses that take place outside the home, for example the theft of a handbag or briefcase, are usually not covered by household insurance, unless the policy contains an 'all risks' extension.

The insurance company may employ experts known as loss assessors and adjusters to process the claim and check on the value of the goods stolen or damaged. It should be noted that household policies rarely cover the full value of money or documents that have been lost.

Even though they have insurance cover, some people do not make a claim for damaged or stolen property. This may be because it is not financially worthwhile, as the policy 'excess' is greater than the value of the loss or because they risk losing a 'no-claim bonus' and premiums might increase or because the claims' procedure is too complex. In this, as in other cases, Victim Support can help by providing practical information and emotional support to help victims cope with the effects of the crime.

Many people are not insured for household loss at all. It is a sad fact that those who are financially vulnerable are more likely to be vulnerable in other ways, including to crime. People who live in high-risk areas may find it impossible to get insurance cover at all, or if they can get insurance, it will only be offered at very high cost. For those who cannot afford insurance, financial difficulties may add considerably to the impact of the crime. For example, television and video equipment, which are often the main items to be stolen, may be rented from – but are not always insured by – a hire company, which may still expect payments to be made.

However, even if no insurance cover is in place, some help may be available, for example a crisis loan or budgeting loan may be available from the benefits' agency to help victims replace essential household items. If children are involved, the local council's social services department may be able to provide an emergency payment. And if the victim is facing extreme hardship, Victim Support may know of charities in the area that may be able to offer second-hand furniture or other help. Citizens' Advice Bureaux also offer a financial advice service. If the victim is a pensioner who has had money they were saving for bills stolen in a burglary, Age Concern may also be able to help. If the victim is not a pensioner and similar money was stolen, utility companies will usually allow people to arrange to pay by instalments, provided that they are made aware of the difficulties.

Other people to contact

If credit cards or cheque books have been stolen, banks and credit card companies must be notified as soon as possible. It is a good idea to telephone first and to follow this up in writing. Similarly, if pension, rent or benefits' books, passports, driving licences, travel cards or bus passes are lost, the issuing authority should also be told.

Some credit card companies and banks now offer protection schemes, under which all credit card, passport and driving licence numbers can be registered for an annual fee. Should these be lost or stolen, all the issuing authorities can be notified quickly as a result of one telephone call.

Claiming compensation

A victim who is injured during a property crime inside or outside their home may be eligible to claim state compensation under the Criminal Injuries Compensation Scheme. There may also be other ways for victims to receive compensation, for example if the offender is ordered to pay compensation if they are caught and found guilty in a criminal court. In addition, if the offender is known, the victim may consider taking out a civil court action against them to claim damages, although it has to be recognised that few offenders will have the financial means to make this worthwhile (see Chapter 2).

Emergency repairs

After a break-in or criminal damage, emergency repairs may be needed to the home. Home-owners will have to arrange this in conjunction with their insurance company. If the victim is a tenant, the landlord, council or housing association should arrange for this to be done immediately. Under the 'right to repair scheme', if it will take a while for long-term repairs to be carried out, the tenant can arrange for minor repairs to be done themselves, and may then be repaid a percentage of what the landlord, council or housing association estimates it would have cost them. However, it is wise to contact the landlord, housing department or association for further information before starting work.

Reducing risk

If keys have been stolen through theft or burglary, locks will have to be changed as a matter of urgency, possibly even to regain entry into the home. But all property crimes usually prompt victims to review their security.

Burglar alarms, window grilles, security lights, deadlocks and window locks – provided they are used – all help to reduce the risk of being burgled. Even the installation of just window locks and deadlocks reduces the risk considerably. This is supported by the *British Crime Survey*, which found that burglars failed to gain entry in more than half of all incidents against households with two or more security devices installed, whereas for households with no security they failed in only one-third of attempts.

Most police forces have a crime prevention officer who can be asked to visit premises and advise about security, and there may also be a community scheme that fits locks and bolts for vulnerable people at reduced or no cost. Victim Support has details of such initiatives and many local schemes are also able to provide direct help themselves. Simple precautions that anyone can take include keeping an inventory of household goods, together with photographs of important items, and marking them with an ultra-violet light sensitive security marker pen. It is a good idea to take action swiftly to guard against the chance of being revictimised in the weeks immediately after the crime.

Although it is important to draw victims' attention to ways in which they might make their homes safer, this should never be presented in a way that increases their anxiety or makes them feel guilty about not having done so earlier. As with any crime, the only person who is responsible is the offender.

Reducing risk for vulnerable people

Older people are often concerned about their vulnerability to crime. While statistics suggest that they are not at significant risk of being burgled, they may be more at risk of burglary by artifice or 'bogus officials' who are only too well aware that older people may keep cash at home.

In addition to the distress that such burglaries may cause, insurance companies may refuse to pay out on claims after this type of crime, because the offender did not break in but was allowed entry by the victim. Older people who keep cash at home should be encouraged to open a post office, bank or building society account as soon as possible.

But it is not just elderly people who are vulnerable to this kind of crime. Children and disabled people who are alone at home are equally at risk and offenders can be very sophisticated in the methods or stories they use to try to gain entry. No stranger should be allowed to enter anyone else's home, no matter on what pretext, without showing identification. The person who answers the door should put the door chain on before opening it and check the caller's identity carefully. If the caller is genuinely from the gas, electricity or water company, for example, they will have an identity card and be able to quote the householder's customer account number, which can be checked.

Other officials should be asked for the telephone number of their office which can be called to verify their identity. If the caller is not an official but someone, for example, who says the house needs repairs, or who wants to buy antique furniture, they should be asked to write and make an appointment. All callers should be kept waiting outside while checks are made, and if there is any doubt about their identity, no caller should be allowed inside. People should especially be suspicious when callers are accompanied.

No-one should feel embarrassed by taking sensible precautions – most callers are genuine and understand the need for them. It can help to make a list of the telephone numbers of all the utility companies and service providers, together with personal account numbers, and keep it by the phone (if they have one) to use in such cases.

Simple ways to help

Many people under-estimate the effect that property crimes may have on their friends and relatives. Those who have read this will be in a position to understand their reactions better and can help by encouraging them to accept the offer of assistance from Victim Support. Victim Support volunteers can provide the practical help and emotional support that victims of property crime may need, for however long they require it.

Other people can help too, for example by listening to the victim and paying attention to what they say about the emotional impact of the crime, as well as the material losses and their significance. While property crimes, with the exception of arson, are rarely life-threatening, they can have a significant psychological impact. It's therefore important not to make assumptions about how anyone will react.

As with all crimes it is important to reassure the victim that the crime is not their fault and that the only person to blame is the offender. It can also be helpful to let them know that most offenders pick victims at random and not by design.

Friends and relatives can also offer practical help to the victim, for example helping them to clean up after the crime, or to notify the issuing authorities about the loss of such things as credit cards and cheque books, or to help them feel safe by discussing how they might improve their security and helping them to achieve this. Being helped to take some sort of action over their safety and security may help the victim in turn to take back control over their life.

7

Crimes Against Children

Overview

- Crimes against children
- How children react to crime
  - The importance of reassurance
  - Bullying
  - Property crimes
  - Violent crimes
  - Child abuse
- Parents' reactions
- What happens after crimes against children
  - Putting crimes against children into context
  - Reporting the crime
  - Victim Support
  - Children in court
  - Criminal injuries compensation
  - Crime prevention
- Simple ways to help

Crimes against children

Most of the crimes referred to here have been discussed earlier in the book and many of their consequences apply to both adults and children. This chapter is about how children may be particularly affected by crime, in the hope that parents and carers will feel better equipped to help them cope with its effects.

A child may be directly affected by a crime that happens to them personally, or indirectly affected if a parent, relative or the whole family is victimised. The crimes most commonly committed directly against children include theft, assault, robbery and sexual offences. The crimes committed against a member of their family or household that most commonly affect children indirectly include burglary, assault and sexual offences. Many of these crimes take place in the context of wider categories of offending behaviour, for example bullying, child abuse, domestic violence and racist violence.

Victim Support normally only sees children under the age of 15 with their parents' or carers' permission. However, some older children and young people may want to seek their own help, for example by telephoning the Victim Supportline on lo-call number 0845 30 30 900 or Childline on 0800 1111.

The crimes against children or affecting children with which Victim Support most often becomes involved are burglary, theft, bullying and assault. Victim Support has trained volunteers who can also provide help in cases of rape and sexual assault, racist violence, domestic violence and murder and manslaughter. In cases of such serious crimes Victim Support will also be able to put child victims and their parents and carers in touch with other organisations who have responsibility in this area.

How children react to crime

In a survey of child victims of crime conducted by Victim Support, 90 per cent of the children who took part said that they had been badly affected by a crime to a greater or lesser degree. Some 55 per cent of the direct victims reported having been very upset by the incident, and of the indirect victims, 80 per cent whose parents were assaulted were very upset, as well as 60 per cent of children in households where there had been a burglary.

Factors that may make it even more difficult for children to cope with crime include their lack of life experience, their emotional and physical vulnerability, and their dependence on adults. A crime may represent the child's first experience of loss and threaten their sense of security at the very moment they are developing their sense of self and of self-confidence.

Children are also physically more vulnerable and less able to protect themselves, either against other children or adults. They may not understand the meaning of the crime, or they may lack the language to describe or conceptualise what occurred. Because they are usually dependent on their parents for where they live and go to school, children may, in addition, be unable to avoid the place where victimisation takes place.

Although, like adults, children's individual reactions to crime vary, the feelings most commonly reported are shock, fear, worry, guilt and anger. Boys are as likely as girls to be upset, and no child is too young to be distressed, although younger children may find it difficult to understand what has happened and explain their feelings. Children within the same family may react differently to the same crime. The emotional effects of crime on children can manifest themselves in physical symptoms, for example headaches, stomach pains, feeling sick or generally unwell.

Behavioural changes associated with crime may include eating or sleeping problems, poor schoolwork, fear of the dark, fear of further crimes, fear of being alone, going upstairs alone or sleeping alone, or regressive behaviour such as 'clinginess' or bed-wetting. They may also refuse to go back to where the crime happened and become withdrawn, or they may react by lashing out or hurting someone or something else. Naturally, how a child reacts will be related to their age and personality.

The effects of indirect victimisation can also be far-reaching. For example, if a parent or sibling has been attacked, a child may refuse to let them out of their sight and become possessive or aggressively protective. If the violence has been sexual and the child is an adolescent, the crime may also affect his or her growing sense of sexual identity.

Whatever the crime, children may find it difficult to tell their parents or carers what has happened, especially if they fear they might get into trouble, or if they feel guilty about the upset it might cause. Neither children nor their parents or carers may realise that these problems are related to the crime, but adopting different behaviours may be the only way that children can show that something serious has happened. Such behaviours are the child's way of dealing with the crime – they are normal reactions to abnormal events. With love and support most children are able to come to terms with their experience and their behavioural symptoms will disappear.

The importance of reassurance

Once they know what has happened to the child and how they feel about it, parents and carers should let children know that they are glad they know now, and not blame them for not telling them earlier. It is important to reassure children that the only person to blame for the crime is the perpetrator and that, as parents or carers, they are more concerned about the child's safety than any loss that may be involved. Even if parents think the child has taken a risk or broken a rule in the time leading up to the crime, they should help children to understand that this did not give the perpetrator the right to, for example, attack or steal from them.

Like all victims, children's ability to recover from a crime is considerably improved if those people closest to them recognise the significance of what has happened and offer appropriate support. Demonstrating this does not mean indulging children with treats to try to make up for the crime, but rather respecting their feelings, acknowledging their distress, and allowing the whole family to be included in the search for a solution.

It is equally important to help children to feel safer following a crime. Keeping as far as possible to family routines will help, but it may also be useful to adopt a 'stepping stone' approach to their recovery. For example, if the child was attacked while playing in a park and the child is fearful of returning to the same spot alone, the parent could first accompany the child there and back again. They could then arrange to take them to the park with friends and collect them later, at a specific time, and this could progress through taking them there, but letting them return alone, or with friends. The final stage is a return to the freedom the child was accustomed to before the crime.

Encouraging children to join a new group or aquire a new skill or sport, so that they can make new friends, may also help to raise their self-esteem.

Bullying

The problem of bullying is widespread and causes children much distress. When it is committed by children against children, bullying is often not thought to be a crime and may even be dismissed by some people as part of 'growing up'. Yet if some of the acts associated with bullying happened to adults, for example harassment, violent attacks, theft and extortion, they would more readily be treated as criminal offences.

As with many crimes, what causes greatest distress is that bullying is a deliberate act in which someone is singled out as the target for a range of behaviours designed to hurt them. It can make children's daily lives a misery and may result in them truanting, running away or even taking their own lives. Bullying can occur in or out of school, among primary as well as secondary schoolchildren, and may be perpetrated by groups or individuals, some of whom may themselves be victims of similar or other crimes.

Signs that a child is being bullied can include reluctance to go to school or go out to play, or evidence that their possessions or money are frequently 'lost'. In such cases, children suffer a second time if they are then blamed by parents or carers for being careless.

If parents or carers suspect a child is being bullied, they should speak to the child's teacher or head teacher. All schools are required to have an anti-bullying policy and parents and carers may therefore discuss this with the school and ask for the school's support in helping their child. Most schools take bullying seriously and will listen to parents' concerns and take action. If they do not, organisations like the NSPCC or ChildLine can offer guidance. Victim Support can also help them to cope with the effects of bullying.

Property crimes

Theft is the most common crime that happens directly to children, and burglary is the most common crime that indirectly affects children as a member of a household.

Bicycles are usually the most expensive items stolen from children, but they may also be robbed of pocket-money or lunch-money, or be bullied into handing over items of clothing, footwear, or precious possessions, such as a personal stereo. As with adults, the significance of the theft may have more to do with what the item represents than its financial value. First possessions are important, and a child who has been given their first pair of football boots as a special present or who has saved for months to buy a new bicycle, may be extremely distressed if they are stolen. This may also be the child's first experience of loss – and of crime – and its impact may be all the greater because, compared with adults, children have fewer possessions to call their own. How that loss is handled may colour and influence their future life.

Children are as much victims of burglary as other family members (see Chapter 6). The strength of their reactions may depend on the circumstances of the crime. For example, children may be particularly affected if they discovered a burglary when they returned home alone after school, or if their room was disturbed in the crime, or if their own possessions were stolen or destroyed.

In such cases, children are often afraid that the burglar will return, particularly at night. It can help if children are included in discussions about home security and in the purchase and fitting of new locks and bolts. Other strategies that may help them feel safer include giving them a personal alarm or a torch so they feel more in control, a night-light to reduce their fear of the dark, or a radio or tape to help them feel less alone. To reassure children that parents are within calling distance, bedroom doors may be left ajar or baby alarms may be reinstalled.

Parents who do not want to encourage their children to become dependent on these devices may prefer to use them temporarily as 'stepping stones' to recovery.

Violent crimes

Children are deeply concerned and anxious about this kind of violence, particularly when it is part of a wider pattern of bullying. As with bullying, this fear may cause victims to truant or feign illness to stay away from school, or to run away from home. Given that children are all too well aware of their state of dependence on adults, such crimes may increase the victim's sense of powerlessness and diminsh their self-confidence and self-esteem. At its most extreme, some children may think that suicide offers their only means of escape.

Some parents can fail to understand the impact that violence has on children and may think that being beaten up by another child represents no more than 'normal' playground fighting or sibling rivalry. It can be useful for parents to think about how they would react if they were physically attacked by a work colleague or relative.

Children can also experience very strong reactions to violent crimes committed against people who are close to them. As with adults, these may include shock and anger at the force used and the hurt caused, and guilt because they could not do anything to help. They may also be frightened of the sight or scale of the injuries, and both anxious about that person's well-being and safety and concerned for their own security, for example worrying about what would happen if the person died.

Children's fears and trauma can be all the greater if they witness the attack, especially if it is as a result of ongoing violent or aggressive behaviour between family members, possibly in the context of domestic violence (see Chapter 5).

Parents and carers who become victims of crime can find it difficult to recognise and deal with children's problems in addition to their own. But it is important to find out exactly what the child is feeling and to allow them to talk about it.

Child abuse

Most people are shocked by reports of children being neglected, beaten or sexually abused. Yet such things do, sadly, happen. To be confronted with such a situation or to have suspicions that it might be happening, is deeply distressing and worrying. The wish to respect a child's confidence or the risk of making a wrong accusation are not easy to deal with.

As with other forms of violence within the home, children may find it difficult or impossible to tell anyone else what is happening. Anyone who is concerned that a child they know may be a victim of any kind of abuse should give the child all the time they want to talk. They should then seek advice from a trusted professional, the NSPCC, ChildLine or local social services.

Like adults, children may find sexual abuse particularly difficult to talk about. Whether it is committed by strangers, acquaintances, carers or family members, children may carry the hurt, shame and guilt associated with the crime alone, and for a long time. It is important for adults to be observant and to listen to children.

The aim of taking action on sexual abuse is to stop the abuse, protect the child from further harm, and to prevent the abuser repeating their crimes against other children. The police, social services or the NSPCC will consider all aspects of the situation carefully before taking action that is aimed at the best interests of the child.

Children who are victims of sexual abuse may above all feel confused. In addition to their general reactions to crime noted earlier, children may feel that what happened was wrong without understanding why. The trauma caused by such crimes, particularly if the abuser is known to, or even a member of, the family, can seem overwhelming for both the victim and their parents and carers. Most child victims of sexual violence therefore need professional help from medical staff who specialise in working with children like them to help them deal with their experience.

Parents' reactions

Just as children suffer deeply from crimes committed against their parents and carers, parents and carers may suffer strong reactions to crimes committed against their children. They may feel guilty that they have failed to protect their child and as a result become possessive or over-protective and set new limits for what the child can and cannot do. Although it may be done out of the best of motives, restricting the child's freedom does little to help their growing sense of independence, which may already have been threatened by the crime. Restricting them further may be interpreted as unjust punishment for a crime that they suffered and did not commit.

Some parents become angry and take action against the offender, and, if they are also a child, against their parents or school. Parents may feel that they have a 'right' to do this, even if the victim protests, and fail to take seriously the risk that the child may suffer additional harm as a result. But this 'right' may also conflict with the child's 'right' to be heard and acknowledged. In such cases, parents' reactions might stand in the way of assisting the child.

The difficulties that parents face when their child has been the victim of sexual abuse are even greater if the perpetrator is a partner or close relative. This can be particularly difficult for parents to believe and may cause rifts in families, especially if the case goes to court and family members feel forced to take sides. The parent may in addition fear financial problems if their partner goes to prison. They may feel jealous that their partner focused their sexual attention on the child, and then guilt that they should have such feelings. In such cases, the child – and/or the parent or carer – may still love the perpetrator and simply want the abuse to stop.

Crimes that happen to children may also awaken painful memories of similar crimes of which parents and carers have been a victim in the past. Such problems are extremely difficult to work through without outside help.

What happens after crimes against children

Putting crimes against children into context

Although the criminal justice system and the media place great emphasis on the role of young people as offenders, many young people are more likely to think of themselves as potential victims. Fear of crime damages children's as well as adults' lives, and if children are to grow up to become law-abiding citizens, they need to know that the law, and society, pays equal attention to their concerns.

A Home Office report which analysed police recorded crime statistics for the period 1990–94 presents disturbing statistics: children under one year old are most at risk of homicide; 22 per cent of rape victims are aged between 10 and 15; over two-thirds of male victims of indecent assault and buggery are aged under 16; and 14 per cent of male victims of assault are aged under 16.

The same report notes that a third of all 12 to 15 year olds said they had been assaulted on at least one occasion in the previous six months, a fifth had had something stolen, a fifth had been harassed by someone their own age, and a fifth by someone aged 16 or more. Seven out of ten young victims had experienced more than one incident.

Reporting the crime

Although deciding whether or not to report crimes to the police may be one of adults' first considerations following a crime, this is not always the case when crimes happen to their children. Parents and carers are more likely to report crimes to the police if the perpetrator is an adult, or if the crime involves theft of a valuable item, possibly because they wish to make an insurance claim. If the perpetrator is also a child, parents are more likely to report incidents of bullying, for example, to the child's school.

In some cases, children will try to stop parents and carers reporting the crimes to anyone, fearing that involving either the police or the school will put them at risk of further harassment or violence. But child victims may be equally concerned and confused if crimes, which they suffer and feel deeply as wrongs, are not reported to anyone. They may feel that no-one, including their parents or carers, takes their suffering seriously, particularly in relation to a crime that would be reported to the police, if it happened to an adult or was perpetrated by an adult. The effects of crime on victims of all ages can be made worse if they are denied both recognition for what they have suffered and support to help them deal with their experience.

Victim Support

Crimes that are reported to the police are usually referred to Victim Support, who will then contact the victim by letter, phone or a visit, to offer help. Crimes involving domestic or sexual violence or crimes that have resulted in a death are only referred with the consent of the person who reports them. Victims of crime can also contact Victim Support themselves, for example by telephoning the Victim Supportline on lo-call number 0845 30 30 900. Other organisations, such as Childline, Kidscape and the NSPCC, provide specialist child services – consult the list at the end of this book.

Many crimes reported to the police by adults are committed against families with children, for example burglaries. Adults in the household may be shocked and frightened themselves and may wish to conceal this. Most children will, however, be acutely aware that something bad has happened. Victim Support can offer help from someone outside the family to sort out practical problems, and to help parents find the best way of dealing with what their children are experiencing, for example by finding ways of being honest about the problems and offering appropriate reassurance.

Children and young people who approach Victim Support themselves will be offered help according to their age and situation, including information about other organisations that may be able to help them.

Children in court

Courts are alarming places for anyone (see Chapter 2), especially for children, but changes have been made to make it easier for them to give evidence in a prosecution. In some courts, judges and barristers remove their wigs and gowns to appear less threatening. Child witnesses should no longer be questioned by the judge to assess whether they know right from wrong, and it should now be left to the jury to decide what weight to give to their evidence.

In cases of violence or sexual violence, children under the age of 17 may not have to go into the courtroom at all. Instead, their evidence may be video-recorded and cross-examination may be done by means of a closed circuit television (CCTV) link. During the cross-examination the child may also be accompanied by a supportive adult, one of whom may be the court usher and the other an independent supporter. Alternatively, the child may sit in court for the cross-examination but speak from behind a screen, provided the judge grants the request, which should be made by the Crown Prosecution Service. Just as an adult witness can re-read their statement before going into court, a child witness may see the video-recording of their first interview before they are cross-examined, to remind them of what they said.

Children need to be prepared for the experience of giving evidence, for example by visiting the court and the CCTV room in advance. However, they must not be 'coached' in the evidence they give. The Witness Service run by Victim Support has staff and volunteers who are trained to offer help to witnesses and their families within the rules of evidence. The Witness Service can also arrange court visits, answer questions, and find the family a private waiting area on the day of the trial. The NSPCC has also published a 'Child Witness Pack', which can be used to explain court procedures to children in a way that is appropriate to their age group.

Criminal injuries compensation

Not reporting crimes to the police severely limits a child's rights to claim compensation through the state-funded criminal injuries compensation scheme for crimes of violence (see Chapter 2). Where the claimant is under the age of 18, claims must be made by an adult with parental responsibility for the child and the child's birth certificate must be enclosed with the claim form. The authority produces a special information sheet for victims of child abuse.

Crime prevention

Some schools have developed peer-group counselling sessions to help children cope with the effects of crime. Others have promoted schemes that spread awareness of how to contact organisations who can help, including Victim Support. All schools are required to have a policy to prevent bullying.

Parents and carers can also take action to try to prevent children from becoming victims of crime. This may range from helping them to security-mark their possessions to helping them to understand more about 'stranger danger', and helping them to develop personal safety strategies to use in a difficult situation. This may include having a coded telephone message that means they want to be collected from wherever they are, fast, with no questions asked, and making sure that they always have with them the money for a taxi fare and the number of a reliable taxi firm.

If parents or carers believe their child is at particular risk of crime, other people, especially teachers, should also be informed. This is particularly important if parents fear their child may be abducted by an ex-partner. In such cases it helps to keep an up-to-date file containing recent photographs of the child and, if possible, of the potential abductor, as well as copies of court orders, birth certificates, medical registration cards and passports. If the child does not have a passport, the parent should write to the Passport Office and lodge an objection to anyone else taking out a passport in the child's name.

Simple ways to help

Although parents and carers may feel that talking to a child about a crime may make things worse, keeping quiet may make them wonder why nothing is being said and may confuse and frighten them even more, allowing their fears to build up over time. Giving truthful answers to the child's questions may help them to deal with the experience all the better.

Listening to children, letting them know they are being listened to, and allowing them to say how they feel is equally important. Children need to know that other people believe what they tell them and don't think that they are lying. This is true for serious allegations and seemingly minor incidents, both of which may reveal a deeper pattern of victimisation.

However, children may need time to come to terms with their feelings and parents and carers should not pressure them into talking if they prefer not to. If they find it difficult to talk about their experience, it can often help to suggest that children draw pictures or write stories about what happened. When parents and carers are trying to encourage children to return to their previous routines and habits, it can be more helpful to do this slowly and in stages.

Children need gentle encouragement and clear, calm, positive and consistent reassurance to give them confidence to overcome the situation. Parents and carers should make sure children understand that they are not responsible for the crime and that they are not being blamed for it.

Parents and carers may also find it productive to include children in crime prevention measures by asking them what can be done to help them feel safer – children will often suggest something that parents and carers have not thought of. Things like night-lights, torches, personal alarms and cassette recorders may all help them to recover their confidence.

Talking to other people about the child's reactions to the crime can also help, particularly to their school. Children's work and/or behaviour may be affected for a time, and teachers may be able to help in the child's recovery if they know the background. If they don't, they might say something out of place.

Getting advice from the family GP or health visitor, or seeking help from Victim Support, might in addition help parents and carers to help their children, and at the same time understand that they and other members of the family may require support in order to cope with the effects of crime.

The following is a brief list of telephone contact details for some of the voluntary and statutory organisations and agencies who can provide information and advice to victims and witnesses of crime.

General advice and information

Victim Support
Voluntary organisation and national association of Victim Support Schemes and Witness Services providing practical help and emotional support to victims and witnesses of crime in England, Wales and Northern Ireland
Tel 0845 30 30 900 (Victim Supportline)

Victim Support Scotland
Victim Support's related organisation in Scotland
Tel 0131 662 4486

Victim Support Republic of Ireland
Victim Support's related organisation in the Republic of Ireland
Tel 00 353 1878 0870

The Samaritans
Voluntary agency providing 24-hour support for people feeling depressed, isolated, or in despair
Tel 0345 90 90 90 (helpline)

National Association of Citizens Advice Bureaux
Voluntary agency providing free and confidential advice through local bureaux
Tel 020 7833 2181

Crime Concern Trust
Voluntary agency working to prevent crime and create safer communities
Tel 01793 863 500

Neighbourhood Watch
Voluntary agency working to help people improve home security and community safety
Tel 020 7772 3348

The police investigation and criminal justice process

Crown Prosecution Service
Government agency with responsibility for prosecuting criminal cases
Tel 020 7796 8500 (central enquiry point)

Police Complaints Authority
Statutory agency responsible for the investigation of serious complaints against the police
Tel 020 7273 6450

Law Society of England and Wales
Governing body of the solicitors' branch of the legal profession in England and Wales
Tel 020 7242 1222

Law Society of Northern Ireland
Governing body of the solicitors' branch of the legal profession in Northern Ireland
Tel 01232 231614

Law Society of Scotland
Governing body of the solicitors' branch of the legal profession in Scotland
Tel 0131 226 7411

The Bar Council
Governing body of the barristers' branch of the legal profession in England and Wales
Tel 020 7242 0082

The Honorary Society of the Inn of Court of Northern Ireland
Governing body of the barristers' branch of the legal profession in Northern Ireland
Tel 01232 241 523

The Faculty of Advocates
Governing body of the barristers' branch of the legal profession in Scotland
Tel 0131 226 5071

National Association for the Care and Resettlement of Offenders (NACRO)
Voluntary agency working to promote the care and resettlement of offenders in the community
Tel 0800 0181 259

Mediation UK
Voluntary agency working to help individuals and organisations to resolve conflict
Tel 0117 904 6661

Criminal Injuries Compensation Authority
Government agency responsible for administering criminal injuries compensation in England, Wales and Scotland
Tel 020 7842 6800

Compensation Agency Northern Ireland
Government agency responsible for administering criminal injuries compensation in Northern Ireland
Tel 028 90 2499 44

Homicide

Support after Murder and Manslaughter (SAMM)
Voluntary agency providing support to families bereaved by homicide
Tel 020 7735 3838

Cruse Bereavement Care
Voluntary agency providing a support service to anyone who has been bereaved
Tel 0345 58 55 65 (bereavement line)

Compassionate Friends
Voluntary agency offering friendship for newly-bereaved parents and grandparents
Tel 0117 953 9639 (helpline)

Sexual violence

Women's Aid Federation
Voluntary agency providing support and temporary refuge for people threatened by violence or abuse
Tel 0345 023 468 (helpline)

Lifeline – Help for Victims of Violence in the Home, Sexual Abuse and Incest
Voluntary agency providing support and advice for families experiencing violence within the home
Tel 01262 469 085

National AIDS helpline
Helpline providing confidential information, advice and support concerning HIV and AIDS
Tel 0800 567 123

Terence Higgins Trust
Voluntary agency offering help and advice for people affected by HIV/AIDS
Tel 020 7242 1010 helpline/020 7405 2381 legal line (both 12 noon to 10 pm)

Crimes against people

Changing Faces
Voluntary agency working with people who have been disfigured, not necessarily as a result of crime
Tel 020 7706 4232

Disabled Living Foundation
Voluntary agency offering information and advice for disabled people
Tel 0870 603 9177 (helpline)

Disability Alliance
Voluntary agency providing training and advice on the welfare rights of disabled people
Tel 020 7247 8776 (enquiry)
  020 7247 8763 (rights advice line)

Alcohol Concern
Voluntary agency providing information on alcohol misuse
Tel 020 7928 7377

Drinkline
National alcohol helpline
Tel 0800 917 8282

The National Drugs Helpline
Helpline providing information and advice on drugs
Tel 0800 77 66 00

MENCAP
Voluntary agency providing advice, support and information to people with a learning disability
Tel 020 7454 0454

MIND
Voluntary agency providing services to help people with mental health problems
Tel 0845 766 0163 (national helpline)

VOICE UK
Telephone helpline for people with learning disabilities who have experienced crime or abuse
Tel 01332 202 555

Age Concern
Voluntary agency promoting the well-being of older people and positive attitudes towards ageing
Tel 0808 808 6060 (helpline)
       0800 00 99 66 (information line: fact sheet 33)

Shelter
Voluntary agency providing advice and assistance to people in housing need
Tel 0808 800 4444 (helpline)

Institute of Race Relations
Conducts research and produces resources to raise awareness of the struggle for racial justice
Tel 020 7837 0041

Commission for Racial Equality
Government agency working to unite Britain for a just society
Tel 020 7828 7022

Lesbian and Gay Switchboard
Voluntary agency providing an information, support and referral service for lesbians and gay men
Tel 020 7837 7324 (helpline)

BT advice line
Offers advice on how to deal with malicious telephone calls
Tel 0800 666700 (malicious calls helpline)
    0800 661441 (nuisance call advisory bureau)

Crimes against children

ChildLine
Voluntary agency providing a telephone counselling service for children and young people in danger and distress
Tel 0800 1111 (helpline)

NSPCC
Voluntary agency working to prevent child abuse and neglect
Tel 0800 800 500 (24-hour Child Protection Helpline)

Kidscape
Voluntary agency working to promote children's safety and prevent child abuse
Tel 020 7730 3300

Reunite (National Council for Abducted Children)
Voluntary agency working to reunite abducted children with their custodial parent
Tel 020 7375 3440 (advice line)

Anti-Bullying Campaign
Voluntary agency working to help parents of children bullied at school
Tel 020 7378 1446

Index